CW00428937

God's Upgraaes . . .
My Adventures

God's Upgrades . . . My Adventures

Learning to Accept and Download

By John Leach

Authentic

Copyright © 2014 John Leach

20 19 18 17 16 15 14   7 6 5 4 3 2 1

First published 2014 by Authentic Media Limited
52 Presley Way, Crownhill, Milton Keynes, MK8 0ES.
authenticmedia.co.uk

The right of John Leach to be identified as the Author of this Work has
been asserted by him in accordance with the Copyright, Designs and Patents
Act 1988.

All rights reserved. No part of this publication may be reproduced, stored
in a retrieval system, or transmitted in any form or by any means, electronic,
mechanical, photocopying, recording or otherwise, without the prior
permission of the publisher or a licence permitting restricted copying.
In the UK such licences are issued by the Copyright Licensing Agency,
Saffron House, 6–10 Kirby Street, London, EC1N 8TS.

British Library Cataloguing in Publication Data
A catalogue record for this book is available from the British Library
ISBN 978-1-86024-912-9
978-1-78078-347-5 (e-book)

Unless otherwise stated, all Scripture quotations are taken from the Holy
Bible, New International Version® (Anglicised edition), © 1979, 1984,
2011 by Biblica (formerly International Bible Society). Used by permission
of Hodder & Stoughton Publishers, an Hachette UK company. All rights
reserved. 'NIV' is a registered trademark of Biblica (formerly International
Bible Society). UK trademark number 1448790.
Scripture quotations marked NRSV are from the New Revised Standard
Version Bible, copyright © 1989 the Division of Christian Education of the
National Council of the Churches of Christ in the United States of America.
Used by permission. All rights reserved.

Cover design by David McNeill (Revo Creative)
Printed and bound by CPI Group (UK) Ltd., Croydon, CR0 4YY

To Chris, Steve, Paul and Vicki,
who have walked this journey with me,
and whose love has been there for better or worse,
in sickness and in health. I'm so proud of you all.

Contents

Foreword

Albert Einstein, asked to account for his life of discovery and intellectual adventure, offered this simple advice: 'The important thing is not to stop questioning . . . Never lose a holy curiosity.' He would have liked John Leach. John's approach to Christian leadership carries three distinctives, each strongly present in this intriguing memoir.

The first is a desire to marry ancient and modern: a living, pulsing, charismatic faith wedded to a deep appreciation for liturgy in all its forms. John has forged a path of renewal that embraces the new with unbridled enthusiasm, but finds joy in the old like a browser at an antiques market.

The second is a searing honesty. If you want a book on leadership that celebrates success but brushes failure under the carpet, don't read this one. John is a leader willing to show his workings. This account of an up-and-down life will encourage you to believe that ministry happens in the real world, not in a parallel universe of air-brushed perfection.

The third is that undimmed curiosity. Hitting his sixties did not make of John Leach a less questioning, less adventurous, more domesticated animal. If anything, age has made him more determined still to seek a faith for the real world. With ever-new challenges to face, his adventure is far from over.

In an age of rapid change with a church in devastating decline and so many of our long-term friends struggling to maintain their faith, we need guides we can trust: travellers who have proved themselves over the long haul. John is one such guide. His feet are firmly on the ground but his heart has never lost its hope and vision. I think I can predict how you will feel as you turn the last page of this book. I think you will be encouraged. I think you will have hope. I think you will find yourself smiling. May God's good hand be on you as you read.

Gerard Kelly

Introduction:
Accept and Download?

I have a philosophy of life. It says that everyone you know, however briefly, leaves you with something that makes your life richer. Even negative people change you, for the better if you let them. It might be quite an insignificant thing: we still use the recipe for leek and potato soup that a parishioner in my first job put in the parish magazine. My ex-brother-in-law was the first person to play me Paul Simon's *Graceland* album: it was my privilege a while ago to attend the twenty-fifth anniversary concert in Hyde Park. Twenty-five years ago? How time flies! Another guy I met at a conference taught me how to do video editing, which I now use all the time. Yet another unknown star was the first person to introduce me to the music of jazz bass virtuoso Brian Bromberg. Little things, but I'd be so much poorer without them.

Sometimes the things that last are not the things you were expecting to last. In one of the many homegroups we have attended over the years we had leaders who faithfully led us in prayer and Bible study week by week. But the really important thing they gave me was cheese. I grew up in a family where my dad just couldn't stand cheese, so there was never any in the house. On the odd occasions I did manage to try any, I had to agree with him: it was gross. But as I grew up and began to realise that there was more to cheese than yellow-orange cuboids of hard Cheddar I became fascinated by all the different shapes, sizes, textures and smells available. I began wistfully to wish that I did like the stuff. I'm like that with tomatoes too: I wish I liked them but I just don't. I spent one Greek holiday with the deliberate aim of getting to like them. I'd heard that if you eat something for long enough you get to enjoy it, and all those Greek salads would give me ample opportunity. But I discovered that the only way I could manage to eat the things was to smother them in tomato ketchup, which made them just about bearable, and also speaks volumes about the relationship between ketchup and real tomato. The net result was that I still hate them, and I spoilt my holiday into the bargain.

Anyway, our homegroup leaders invited us round for a meal, and out came the cheeseboard at the end. I confessed my sad inability to eat the stuff, but my wish that I could, and with the infinite care and patience that only good homegroup leaders can muster, they suggested I might try a little bit of *this* one, as it didn't really taste much like cheese. So I tried my first-ever crumb of that Austrian smoked stuff, which looks like a little brown plastic sausage and, much to my delight, it wasn't half bad. That moment was a turning point for me, and I began to explore, and eventually get to love, the rich variety of cheesy comestibles that God, in his bounty, has put into our world. Peter and Elizabeth: you changed my life!

Less successful but equally significant for me was a couple, whose names I can't even remember any more, who were in the next tent to us on a French camping holiday. We struck up a friendship with them, and were invited round to their tent the next evening for a meal. 'I'll do you mussels', she told us. Oh dear! That was a problem because if there was one thing I hated even more than cheese it was anything in a shell. I'm an Essex boy and, throughout my childhood, every Sunday teatime without fail we had pints of stinky, slimy, vinegar-soaked filter-feeding molluscs, fresh from the cockle stalls of Leigh-on-Sea. I completely failed to see how anyone in their right mind could bring themselves to eat any of the stuff, and even to enjoy it to the degree that they ate some every week. I reckon that the one big unanswered question, which puts all the other mysteries of the universe into the shade, is this: who was the first person ever to eat a whelk? And what on earth made them do it? Fortunately there was always Spam as an alternative for the wayward son who had yet to appreciate the joys of seafood, but I grew up with a profound disgust of all things in shells. And now our neighbours were having us round for mussels.

I felt I had no choice but to confess. 'What is it you don't like about them?' she asked me. 'The taste? The texture?'

'I don't know,' I explained. 'I've no idea what they taste or feel like. I've never tried one. Put one of those in my mouth? You must be joking!'

Her memorable words ring down the years: 'You *will* like them the way I cook them!' So the next evening, and we have a photo to record this milestone event, I ate my first-ever mussel.

I made an important discovery that day: I'd been right all along. They were every bit as disgusting as I had feared they would be. But at least now I could say I'd tried them. I love telling this story to people who tell me that the Bible is a load of rubbish. They've never read any of it, but they just know it's rubbish. But whoever and wherever that couple are now, you allowed me to hate mussels *after* trying them. You gave me integrity in garlic sauce.

Some gifts from people are even more significant. I'm writing this in the team lounge at Spring Harvest, an annual Christian festival at which it has been my privilege to speak for the last few years. This year I bumped into a guy who was in my youth group in my first curacy thirty-two years ago. It was he who nagged me relentlessly to go to Spring Harvest and, when we finally gave in, it was quite literally life-changing. We had reached rock bottom in our difficult first years of ordained ministry, and I was ready to give it all up and go and find a proper job. But Spring Harvest turned me round, re-envisioned me and sent me back into the fray, which is why I count it such a privilege to be able to be on the team now, maybe doing for others what was done for me all those years ago. But without the nagging of that teenager I don't think we'd ever have bothered, and who knows where I'd be today? It really was great to meet up with him again.

I can also remember the first time I heard about e-mail. Roger Jones, he of Christian musicals fame, was telling me that you could send letters to as many people as you liked, instantly, at absolutely no cost and with no need at all for stamps. Much as I liked and trusted Roger, I simply couldn't believe that this was possible. I thought he was winding me up. It was some years later that I discovered the joys of the digital revolution for myself. I don't consider myself a

Luddite, but I simply found it impossible to believe that such technology existed.

I think also of another homegroup leader who we met up with recently after having nearly lost touch. She had lost loads of weight, and told us about the particular diet that had worked so well for her. Her throwaway comment 'I'm much better at abstinence than I am at moderation' instantly struck a chord in me, and over the next year I lost five and a half stone, and subsequently ran my first-ever five kilometre race. Before that I'd struggled to lumber five yards.[1]

There are so many people who have in all sorts of ways, significant or not, enriched my life. I could tell you so many: my Old Testament tutor at college who, even though he insisted in lecturing with his little finger wedged firmly in the corner of his mouth, nurtured in me a profound love for the Old Testament, which I personally have enjoyed reading and preaching on much more than I have the New. The group of people who first introduced me to single malts, another friend who taught me all I know about creative liturgy and worship, the chance comment from a publisher that launched my writing career, the person who first recommended to me The Ragley Boat Stop, a pub near Derby where you can eat your own weight in steak, my mate who finally nudged me to take the Institute of Advanced Motorists (IAM) advanced driving course that I'd been meaning to do for forty years . . . (By the way *everyone* should do the driving course. It cost £139 and saved me nearly £200 in car insurance in the first year alone. Apparently I'm 70 per cent less likely to have a prang now, than I was before I passed.)

But this book is about something bigger than music, cheese or driving. If individuals, and some of them like ships passing in the night, can leave me with so much, weaving into my life things that have left me different and for which I remain profoundly grateful, how much more have I seen God weave into my life? And how much greater is the possibility of change and newness when God meets us and puts into our lives things for which we remain profoundly grateful?

That's what this book is about. God has a plan for constant product improvement, or 'sanctification' as the theologians like to put it. It's like your favourite piece of computer software: you click to use it one day and a little window comes up telling you that they've produced a better version, which has got rid of some of the less-than-helpful features of the one you're currently using. Sometimes I feel quite happy with what I have, and don't really feel the need for anything more complicated. But at other times I'll gladly accept and download the newer version.

God's Research and Development Engineer, or 'The Holy Spirit' as he's known, is constantly offering us upgrades. I want to tell you about some of the ones I've had installed, not because I've yet reached that elusive bug-free state of perfection (far from it!) or even because I think you'll be that interested in my little life, but because there might be things about which I can reassure you, and encourage you to accept and download what God is upgrading in your own. Maybe this book is a bit like one of those on-line forums where we can learn from the experience of others. God doesn't, of course, send a global new release all around the world at the same time: that's where my software analogy breaks down. He is a loving father, not a geek in a lab somewhere, and he deals with all his children as individuals, putting into our lives at different times just the fixes we need at that moment. I want to encourage you to be aware of what he might be doing in your life, so that you can accept and download it.

I do need to say one more thing though, something that the Bible itself makes very clear, and which writers on 'spirituality' (the way we relate to our God) have always known and, again, this will be a departure from any kind of computer analogy. It is this: God seems to upgrade us far more often and more thoroughly through suffering and hardship than during the good times. Software manufacturers try to make it as easy as possible for us to upgrade: God seems to have chosen a different way. So many of the stories in this book will be about pain, struggle and bad times. Yet I have found it to be the case that it is in those times that the most thorough upgrading goes on. In one of the many references to this dynamic in the New Testament, Paul wrote in Romans 5:3–4:

> We also glory in our sufferings, because we know that suffering produces perseverance; perseverance, character; and character, hope.

James also wrote about this same dynamic:

> Consider it pure joy, my brothers and sisters, whenever you face trials of many kinds, because you know that the testing of your faith produces perseverance. Let perseverance finish its work so that you may be mature and complete, not lacking anything (Jas 1:2–4).

It was C.S. Lewis who wrote about God whispering to us in our pleasures, speaking to us in our conscience, but shouting in our pains – that these pains are, in effect, God's megaphone to rouse a deaf world.[2]

Richard Rohr, a Franciscan priest from New Mexico, wrote a highly insightful book about this dynamic of growth through suffering and failure.[3] He quotes psychologist Carl Jung who says that so much unnecessary suffering comes from people's unwillingness to accept what he calls the 'legitimate suffering', which comes simply through being human. Life is hard, and when we try to deny that we're heading for a fall. But to see suffering as a redemptive gift from God can give us a whole new take on it. It's not necessarily any less painful, but it does give it a sense of purpose, and an awareness that God is at work through it.

One of the ways in which God gets our attention is through the gift of discontent. Think for a moment about when you change your car, or redecorate your lounge, or buy a new carpet. Almost certainly it is when the old one is no longer working, or has become tired, grubby or threadbare. I learnt fairly early on in ministry that the job of a leader wanting to help people to change is first of all to make them unhappy. While everything is fine and working well no-one sees any need for change. So given the helpful definition of a leader as one who 'defines reality', it is often our task to help people see that in fact things could be so much better. When you've lived with a threadbare carpet for a while you stop noticing it, and it can take a friend to point out to you gently that it might well be time for a change. I have also found over the years that if the role of a leader is to make people unhappy, I have a tremendous anointing for it!

I once attended a brilliant seminar called 'The Spiritual Gift of Dissatisfaction' by Bishop Graham Cray at New Wine.[4] He made the point that the Holy Spirit is the one who draws us towards the future, the deposit guaranteeing our inheritance, as Ephesians 1 puts it. But he is also the one who drives us out into mission in the real world as it is now, equipping us to roll up our sleeves and walk amongst the poor, broken and hurting. This dual work of the Spirit, said Graham, can feel as though we're being stretched on one of those medieval torture racks. Everything within us wants to let go, if we could, of either one end or the other. Thus some Christians live in the triumphalistic world of the future, singing songs of glory and losing touch with the real world now. Others let go of the other end, become immersed in pain and suffering, and lose hope, descending into anger and cynicism. It is the work of the Spirit to help us stay attached at both ends, and it is our work to listen to our painful feelings of discontentment and recognise them as the voice of God to us. So at various times in my story you'll hear this voice of frustration, a nagging sense that things aren't quite right. I think I have learnt, or am trying to learn, that this discomfort is a gift for me from God, because he is wanting to lead me towards another breakthrough, another upgrade.

I hope this won't be a miserable book, though. The secret, which at my ripe old age I'm just beginning to learn, is to get some kind of understanding of the fact that our pains aren't just some random rotten tomatoes thrown at us by a cruel world. They can be the gifts of a loving Father God who

wants us to be the best he made us to be. Isaiah 49 contains a
passage that is typical of several others of a similar vein:

> Listen to me, you islands;
>   hear this, you distant nations:
> Before I was born the LORD called me;
>   from my mother's womb he has spoken my name.
> He made my mouth like a sharpened sword,
>   in the shadow of his hand he hid me;
> he made me into a polished arrow
>   and concealed me in his quiver.
> He said to me, 'You are my servant,
>   Israel, in whom I will display my splendour.'
> But I said, 'I have laboured in vain;
>   I have spent my strength for nothing at all.
> Yet what is due to me is in the LORD's hand,
>   and my reward is with my God.'
> And now the LORD says –
>   he who formed me in the womb to be his servant
> to bring Jacob back to him
>   and gather Israel to himself,
> for I am honoured in the eyes of the LORD
>   and my God has been my strength –
> he says:
> 'It is too small a thing for you to be my servant
>   to restore the tribes of Jacob
>   and bring back those of Israel I have kept.
> I will also make you a light for the Gentiles,
>   that my salvation may reach to the ends of the earth'
>   (Isa. 49:1–6).

Isaiah tells of God's plan to prepare his servant Israel for the task he has for her. Much of this goes on in the secret places, where God is polishing, honing and sharpening his tools ready for the job which lies ahead. Verse 4 gives us a bit of insight from Israel's point of view: 'What is going on here? What have I achieved, and why does it seem so worthless? Oh well, it's up to God to reward me I suppose.' But then comes the really stunning truth: God has a plan, so secret yet built in from day one, and so much greater and more significant than Israel could have imagined. God's plan is nothing short of world domination!

Of course this has always been God's plan. The whole story started when he called Abraham to a two-fold task: to be blessed, and then to be a blessing to others. That was back in Genesis 12. Yet it has been a major fault of his people since then that they have so often wanted the first bit without the second. This principle came home to me with stark clarity a few years ago, when my wife Chris and I had London theatre tickets for something or other, and we thought it would be nice to have a meal before the show. We found a restaurant, part of a well-known chain, and ordered our meal. If things had kept going as they were we would have time for some afters and then a quick walk to the theatre just round the corner. The food was very nice, but when we'd finished the main course, things came to an abrupt halt. It wasn't that we couldn't catch the eye of a waiter or waitress: we couldn't even catch sight of one. For over twenty minutes we sat and waited, until the point where afters were totally out of the question: if we didn't go right then we'd have missed the play as well. Eventually in desperation I got up and went to explore. In a dark booth at the back of the restaurant I found a large table full of uniformed waiting staff, all tucking into a convivial meal together.

'I'm so sorry to interrupt your dinner,' I told them, 'but I really need to get my bill and get to the theatre.' Reluctantly one of the group detached himself and with a surly look got my bill.

On the positive side it did save me money on a tip, but I reflected with Chris on this experience as being a deeply theological one. In the Old Testament (and subsequently) the Jews were very proud of being 'God's chosen people', but they constantly forgot the fact that they were chosen to be waiters and waitresses of the good things of God, serving them up to everyone else. Yet so often their history was one of wanting blessing but not wanting to bless others; of sitting and eating by themselves while others went hungry. So throughout the Old Testament there are reminders from God of what it really means to be a chosen person: Isaiah 49 is one of those. Sadly this colossal missing of the point continued into the New Testament. Just look at the work God had to do in the early chapters of Acts to convince the Christians that Jesus wasn't just for Jewish people! And of course this tension is as rife as ever in the Christian church today, as we so easily fall into the mindset of thinking it is all about us having the nice times of worship or whatever exactly as we like them. Meanwhile others are longing to be fed while we party. This is a tension that is going to get me into trouble before the end of this book, but more of that later.

Ever felt that your life is a random succession of things happening to you? That your attempts to live for God are pretty worthless, considering the effort it all costs you? Well, it might just be that God is working away on you, in some places that are hard to see at the moment, and that he is sharpening and polishing you because the task he has for you is something that at the moment feels unbelievable, but has actually been built in to his purposes right from the beginning. I believe that passages like the one in Isaiah are in the Bible because God wants us to understand this dynamic, and to co-operate with him in it.

A new version of you is available: a significant improvement that can do so much more, and do it so much more effectively, than ever before.

But God doesn't just download: we have to accept.

1

Early Days

Like most people I have all sorts of vague 'memories' from my early childhood, mainly because people have told me about them rather than because I can actually remember them. I don't think my dad was in any sense a villain, but he was a bit of an East End lad, and would sometimes, though not often, recount tales of mischief from his days in Bethnal Green, from where, being in an upwardly mobile family, they moved to Dagenham Heathway. He met my mum, a somewhat nominal Baptist, at work in his drawing office, and two years after they married I came along. My sister was born three years later and, much later still, at our request, my brother joined us.

But when I was 5, life changed dramatically. Through some friends at work my dad became a Christian. They had been nagging away at him for some while, apparently, and one day he finally caved in. I still have his Bible, which tells me inside the front cover that this Damascus Road conversion occurred on 1 August 1957, and, although it doesn't say so in the Bible, he told me that it was at 10:50 p.m.

As a minister with over thirty years' experience I know that nowadays far more people come to faith gradually than in a flashing moment of insight or surrender, and I also know that so many so-called 'conversions' never really 'take'. But for my dad the seed had obviously fallen on the good soil, and from that moment life changed dramatically. I'm not desperately keen on the way the term 'born again' has been hijacked and used as a pejorative description of real Christians, but in his case it could be applied perfectly aptly.

We began to go to the Baptist church to which my mum had been somewhat notionally attached, and from day one we were in at the deep end, attending two services each Sunday as well as Sunday afternoon Sunday school. This pattern continued for the next thirteen years until I left home. It never occurred to me to rebel and try to stay in bed, and in any case I simply would not have been allowed to. This was what we did, and to try not to do it was as unthinkable as trying not to go to school five other days of the week. And it wasn't all bad. My favourite bit was the sermon, because I knew that for the next forty minutes I was going to snuggle up uninterrupted to my mum. Virtually all of it went well over my head, but I loved those times of closeness, and felt happy and secure in church.

My dad's faith came alive, and so did my mum's, and until his death in 2006 my dad remained a member of that same church, serving at different times as a deacon and an elder, preaching and leading worship, engaging in study groups, pastoral visits . . . you name it. His was a faith that he really meant and lived, and the whole family took their cue from him. He was one of the most gifted personal evangelists I have ever known: many of his drawing office staff became Christians, and at his standing-room-only funeral I looked around and saw countless people who are now living for God as a result of his witness.

The other great legacy he left me was DIY. He was a very practical man, trained as an electrician and a plasterer. My granddad was a professional painter and decorator, and he has passed on those skills too. I wouldn't claim to be anywhere near as proficient as my dad was, but it has been a great delight to me to pass on to my own kids some of the useful household skills I picked up from him. I know nowadays you're not supposed to do even the smallest electrical job without paying a proper electrician to check it afterwards for you, but the ability to do some basic household jobs myself has been a joy to me and useful to others whom I have been able to help practically. One or two near misses have also taught me a profound respect for mains electricity, which is a useful life lesson. A couple of times I nearly had more of an upgrade than I was expecting.

So what did I learn about God in those early years? This is going to be difficult for me to write about, because I can easily give you the wrong impression, about my church in particular and the denomination of which it was a part. So I do need to say that these were basically happy years, and the church was full of good, well-meaning, committed Christian disciples, led by godly and wise men (yes, it was men). But I can only report what I, as a child and then a teenager, picked up and understood. Sadly the God whom I believed in and sought to follow was basically not very nice.

First of all he didn't like us doing anything, and especially not on Sundays. Fun was banned, as were things like ice cream. We weren't allowed to do anything that remotely involved shopping, not that there was much opportunity a) because shops didn't open in those days, and b) because there would have been no time anyway, as we spent most of the day at church. As children we had to be quiet, because Sunday was a day of rest, and I've already told you about the shellfish, although I don't think to be honest that that had much to do with God. But it all added to the general unpleasantness of the day.

Then there were the other sins. People who smoked, drank, swore or gambled were beyond the pale, and were severely looked down upon by us good Christians. The job of parents was to protect their children from any encounter with such activities. I can remember during my Beatles phase leaving the sheet music for 'Sexy Sadie' on the piano. When it was discovered there was a major row, and the offending music had to be removed from the house lest it polluted us all with the 'S' word. We also had to be protected from the harsher realities of church life. I can remember our organist resigning and leaving the church, accompanied by many sage looks and shaking of heads. Only many years later did I discover that this was over some crisis of faith, but it clearly wasn't something to be shared with the youngsters. It could have done us real harm.

Don't get the wrong idea: my family were basically loving and committed to God, and genuinely wanted the best for us. Most of the time we got along fine. But with hindsight the God whom we sought to follow was fundamentally a God who didn't want us to do things. I developed the belief (and please understand me that I now realise that this is not official

Baptist doctrine) that your eternal destiny, heaven or hell, depended entirely on what you happened to be doing at the moment of Jesus' return. As you can imagine this led to a somewhat insecure faith, although the upside was that I did learn to sin very quickly and get it over with. But the clear message was that you could only please God by not doing stuff.

What then of Jesus? The Jesus of my childhood was the master of the clever put-down. We delighted in him getting one over on the nasty scribes and Pharisees, and much of the preaching I can remember was about how we might do the same and win arguments with non-Christians. This was important, because the one thing God did want us to do was personal evangelism. We had to win other souls to Jesus, and we had to know how to do it. Our strategy consisted firstly of showing people the right Bible verses, which explained 'The Way of Salvation', and then winning arguments over those who were not fully convinced by our Bibles. I can remember trying to stuff an old Authorised Version Bible into my school-shorts pocket because my friend Graham needed witnessing to, since he had said a rude word in the playground. I took him through Romans 3:23 ('all have sinned'), Romans 6:23 ('the wages of sin is death'), John 3:16 and many other verses. Sadly he seemed unimpressed, although I hope something might have gone in because he died a few years later of pernicious anaemia.

Keeping it Trinitarian, what did I learn of the Holy Spirit during these formative years? Absolutely nothing, apart from the fact that he featured in 'The Grace', which is what most meetings ended with.

As you might expect in our denomination, baptism was seen as a big deal. The basic position was, and as far as I am aware remains for Baptists, that you are guilty until proven innocent; that is, you are not a child of God unless you deliberately opt in and decide to become one. This applies across the age range, so the job of both parents and Sunday school teachers was an evangelistic one: children had to reach the point of becoming Christians. This is in stark contrast to the Anglican position, where children of Christian parents are considered 'in' unless at some point they deliberately opt out, and are therefore quite appropriately baptised as babies. Children's ministry Anglican-style is much more about nurture than evangelism. In the Baptist church I grew up in you could become a Christian at any age, but you weren't allowed to be baptised until you had reached 'the age of understanding', clearly a significant age, although to this day no-one has been able to tell me when it is. At special times during the year the 'Decision Book' was brought out, and anyone who had decided to become a Christian could sign their name in it. One key event in the church calendar was the Sunday School Anniversary weekend, when a special preacher would come and urge us all to make a decision for Christ. I signed the book when I was 7, although I can't now remember what prompted this radical step. There was great rejoicing, like unto that over a sinner repenting. But after that nothing changed, of course, since I was already trying my best to avoid all the sins that would upset God if he caught me doing them.

As far as I could tell, the theology of baptism was very simple in our Baptist church: it was nailing your colours to the mast. It was about a public witness that from now on we were going God's way. A key text (which in context has nothing whatsoever to do with baptism) was from Joshua 24:15: 'Choose for yourselves this day whom you will serve . . . as for me and my household, we will serve the LORD.'

On this text hung many a classic baptism service sermon: we all have to make a choice whom we will serve, to whom we will dedicate our lives. X is here in this service to say that as for him/her, that commitment is to Jesus. How about you? Come forward during the last hymn if you want to say that too. (I now find it interesting that the 'me and my household' bit, which is a major plank of Anglican baptismal theology, never seemed to be pursued with quite the same theological vigour. In true Enlightenment style, baptism was, and could only ever be, an individual choice.)

I knew that sooner or later I would have to give in and get baptised, not least for the joy it would give everyone else, but it became a battle of wills. Since following God meant not doing anything evil, and since as I grew up I understood more and more of the delicious possibilities of life, baptism seemed a bit of a risky thing to do. To nail my colours to the mast, go public and say from now on I was going to be a good boy seemed a big ask. I was bound to set myself up for a crashing failure. So I resisted with all my might. It had also become a competitive sport: I had joined the Scout Group when I was 13, and a group of us became great friends. We all attended church regularly: it was definitely a church-based group, led by Christians, but we were all feeling the pressure to get baptised, and were all equally hesitant. On Sunday nights we would buy a bottle of beer each (although I had coke as I couldn't stand the stuff), retire to my grandma's (she was a lot more liberal than my parents when it came to alcohol) and hold profound theological discussions. There didn't seem to be any forum within the life of the church for raising or discussing difficult questions, so we had to do it ourselves.

Finally, during one particularly emotional appeal at church, I could stand it no longer. I gave in, got up out of my seat, went down the front and expressed my wish to get baptised, much to the surprise of my friends who remained firmly in their pews. As far as I know they have never taken their relationships with God any further. My baptism eventually happened one Sunday shortly before I left home for university and jacked the whole lot in, but more of that later.

Why am I telling you all this? Because at one of our church staff meetings a while ago we had a discussion started by someone who admitted that he had grown up with the belief that God didn't like him very much, and only grudgingly had anything to do with him. As we talked several of us in the room admitted to exactly the same feelings, and we noted that the majority of us had been brought up in free church backgrounds. After a while someone asked the question 'What happened to change you? How did you come to accept that God loves you, is for you, and values you?' I pondered this, and eventually answered, 'When I became an Anglican.'

Let me say two things about this. First of all, as I have said, I am not writing to knock another denomination, its beliefs or practices. Some of my best friends are Baptists, and I have no doubt that the childish impressions of God and faith that I managed to pick up are a million miles from any kind of official Baptist belief. I am also aware that times have changed since I was a teenager, and churches of all stripes have perhaps lost a bit of the hard edge, and realised that in our culture evangelism, for example, works very differently (sadly not everyone has learnt this lesson, but most have). So I'm not in any way wanting to say that Anglicans have got it right while Baptists have got it wrong. I'm very aware that as a denomination mine isn't exactly a shining example of orthodox faith and effective ministry.

But the second thing I want to say is that you might have picked up the same impressions that I did when you were young. You may have misunderstood God and the gospel as badly as I did, and you may be living still with the sense that God only grudgingly endures your feeble attempts at worship and Christian living. You may be hoping for the best when it comes to heaven, but without any great degree of certainty or security. If you were asked the question, 'How did you come to accept that God loves you, is for you, and values you?' you might perhaps answer: 'I haven't!'

I needed a serious upgrade to this bug-infested faith. But before I got to that I had to crash completely.

2

The God Who Speaks

In spite of the rather negative-sounding spiritual upbringing I have been describing, I had on one occasion 'encountered' God. I wouldn't have used that language at the time, but with hindsight this, my first real spiritual experience, was the forerunner of many with which my life has been peppered. But more of that later. My first real sense of the presence of God was on a school trip to France. We were a small group, just six pupils and three teachers, our French teacher, the art master who was sweet on her (and later married her) and the RE teacher who had been in France during World War II and who therefore spoke the language passably if not fluently. Being such a small group we hired a somewhat unreliable Commer van, which we christened *Le Van Bleu*, and which was most decidedly a *van ordinaire*. Among the pupils was Frances, the love of my life, but we never really managed to get it together, and she felt it certainly wouldn't have been fair to have a holiday romance in those circumstances, and amongst such a small group. We had a great time, but I was also struggling with my unrequited love and the kind of teenage existential angst that is *de rigeur* for sensitive 16-year-olds like me.

I can remember walking back from a café in Avignon where we were staying with Mr Robinson, the RE teacher, and asking him what he thought the purpose of life was. I think I must have been in the mood for some kind of theological debate, but his answer was instant, straightforward and clear: it is to find the will of God for you and do it. That didn't leave me a lot to argue about, but I've never forgotten his take on the meaning of life, and have myself dished it out to others on many occasions.

A few days later we took *Le Van Bleu* and visited the beautiful city of Aix-en-Provence. It was a scorchingly hot day, and my friend George and I took refuge in the cool cathedral, and had a few minutes' sit down. As cathedrals go it was a bit of a dowdy affair, somewhat lacking in colour or décor. We sat down near the front and were looking at the high altar, when suddenly the sun must have come out from behind a bit of cloud, because the altar was unexpectedly bathed in light and colour. At that precise moment the organ started to play, all high-pitched and angelic. After a while George articulated the question I think we'd both been asking ourselves: 'Can you hear the organ playing?' It seemed a silly question, but we were both absolutely rapt, each thinking that the music was some kind of angelic serenade just for our own ears. We sat together in silence for a few minutes until the moment passed, but that incident has stayed with me as the time when I knew beyond any doubt that God really is there, a belief that I have held unwaveringly ever since – apart from one week in 1986 (that's another story). I had felt emotional a few times in church, of course, but this was not mere emotion: this was God. There was no-one up the front telling me what I was supposed to be feeling; there was no emotional hymn singing or hype of any kind. God had just chosen to visit us in that moment.

I'm aware that in the telling it doesn't sound all that, but, with the background I've given, you can perhaps begin to see that I was discovering something (or rather someone) new. This was a God whom it felt good to meet, really good. But it was to be a few years until I met him again.

Shortly after my baptism I left home to go to York University to read Chemistry and Education. I suppose you could say I had led a sheltered existence, so to be away from home for the first time was quite an experience. I loved both the city and the university campus, and I quickly made some great friends. I discovered that university friends were unlike school friends: they didn't seem to be capable of the cruelty that I had sometimes experienced before. It was a chance to start again where nobody knew anything about me other than what I chose to tell them, so we all started on an equal playing field. I also discovered girls. At school I had been the shy little boy with glasses who was always the last to get chosen when picking sides for football, and my romances, like that with Frances, never really got off the ground. But at York I was as eligible as anyone else. It was a great time, and if I were writing an autobiography rather than a spiritual narrative I could tell you many, many tales. However, I must just indulge myself briefly and tell you about some of my chums, since it was they who made this time so significant for me.

Steve the Heap was from Hampshire somewhere. He was tall, blond, quiet and the most accident-prone person I have ever met. Everything he touched fell to bits. There was a dent in the plasterboard of his room next to the light switch where he had missed one night. One day on a trip to an antique shop he had knocked over an oil painting and put his foot through it, before wandering off to cause some other devastation elsewhere in the shop. On another occasion he just walked past a Reliant Robin parked by the kerb and the door fell off. He never walked down stairs: he skied down on the points of the steps with his enormous feet, usually managing a graceful landing at the bottom, although on one occasion, on some steps down to the riverbank in York, he made the mistake of attempting this descent while carrying his flageolet (a kind of tin whistle that was his musical instrument of choice). It ended up embedded in the palm of his hand like an apple corer when he slipped more rapidly than anticipated.

Steve was a member of the party that often went on what we called 'Rubinds'. These were ceremonial walks to York station, along a set route, with various activities along the way. One red phone box was the site for a bout of 'Rabbentaft', a newly created form of martial art where any physical contact with one's opponent was forbidden, and I seem to remember a certain tree along the way that we had to swing from. But the ultimate Rubind destination was the station buffet, which was the only place where you could get a tea and a snack at any time of day or night. It was on one of the station platforms, so you had to buy 'platform tickets', which cost 2d (less than 1p today) and allowed you onto the platform but not onto any train. The buffet was also a good source of plastic teaspoons, which were in short supply in university halls of residence. On one occasion Steve had accumulated loads of them, gleaned from repeated trips to the condiments section of the buffet, and had secreted them up the sleeve of his army greatcoat. All was going well, until we were exiting the barrier and had to give in our platform tickets. Steve had forgotten to get his out of his pocket, and instinctively dropped his arm to reach for it, at which point forty plastic spoons clattered onto the floor in front of the bemused ticket collector. I can't remember how we made our excuses and left, but I'll remember Steve's face, and that of the British Rail man, to the end of my days.

Then there was Pete, who was so sickeningly good-looking that he had a constant stream of beautiful girlfriends. He was one of those people who seem to have a golden touch on life: he was being sponsored through university by Rolls-Royce, so was never short of money. Jess had worked as a bus conductor in his native Wolverhampton, and still wore the uniform daily to prove it, such that the staff on York buses always refused to take any money from him. He had a wild shock of Afro hair, and every time he washed it he found several unsmoked cigarettes that he had secreted in there for later. Two other friends were unhelpfully both called Rod, but their hairstyles were so different that it was easier to refer to them as Curly Rod and Long Straight Rod.

My time in York was one of tremendous fun, but at a much deeper level I enjoyed profound acceptance, the like of which I had never known before. I don't know whether that had been due to the somewhat oppressive spiritual upbringing, or my own defective personality, but it was only now, for the first time, that I felt I was among equals. I knew I was loved and valued by my friends, each of whom has left me something. I'm sure God used the experience to upload into me a much more healthy sense of who I was, and what I had to offer.

One of the important personal gifts that was given to me during this period was one that was going to become hugely significant for me later. Pam was one of those naturally posh people who wear it well, and don't need to pose or prove anything, so she fitted well with the rest of us plebs. Her parents lived in a huge house in Middlesex and had a grand piano autographed by Sir Henry Wood (whoever he was, but I was obviously meant to be impressed, so I went along with it). One day Pam asked me if I was interested in going to a prom, as she had a couple of tickets.

Now at this stage I knew all about music: it was Keith Emerson. The Nice had just given way to Emerson Lake & Palmer, and I was their number one groupie. So once I had ascertained that a 'prom' was in fact just a gig for posh people, I said I was up for it. I asked which bands were playing and apparently there was one called 'Beethoven'. I'd never heard of them, and to be honest didn't think they sounded promising, although the album they'd be featuring was called (and I think I heard her correctly) 'The Erotica Symphony'. So what was there not to like?

A few months later we turned up at this huge club in London called the Albert Hall. There was a bit of a queue to get in, and it was standing room only in the mosh pit, but everyone seemed very pleasant, if, like Pam, a bit posh. Apparently before Beethoven took to the stage there was the statutory support band, an outfit completely unknown to me called 'Berlioz', who were going to perform an album unpromisingly entitled 'Tedium'. Still, that was how it was in those days: I'd sat through hours of 'Third Ear Band' kind of stuff before the real music started, so I settled down to wait for the action to begin.

I don't know if you've ever heard Berlioz's *Te Deum*[5] but if you have you'll have heard one of the most dramatic openings to any piece of classical music ever. For the next forty-five minutes I sat spellbound with my jaw dropped open listening to just about the most stunning music I'd ever heard in my life. I was an instant and total convert, and even Beethoven turned out to be rubbish in comparison. As Pam and I walked out into the warm summer Kensington air at the end of the evening, I made a vow to myself: before I die I'm going to hear that magnificent work performed again. And if I'm rich enough by the time I do die, I'm going to have it at my funeral. Pam's little gift into my life had been a huge one.

In spite of the fun, laughter and general tomfoolery of those days I knew the importance of keeping my Christian life going, and I had every intention of going along to the Baptist church in York. It's just that it never actually happened. There was so much to do that was far more fun, and Sunday mornings certainly weren't made for getting up early, getting dressed up and sneaking out before anyone else saw you, to go to church. Every week it was on my list of good intentions, but sadly the attractions of sex and drugs and rock and roll proved too strong. And of course because I didn't go I felt guilty, and I felt even more guilty because of *why* I didn't go.

I never stopped believing in God, and I certainly never deliberately turned my back on him. There were just better things to do. Just before we broke up for Christmas a few of us decided to go to the Carols by Candlelight service in the local parish church. But hopes that my dormant faith might be rekindled by a visit to God's house were shattered when one of our party had a sudden and noisy attack of flatulence that just wouldn't go away. We giggled our way through the service like silly schoolchildren, hoping that the eruptions would come during the carol singing and not during some silent period of prayer. We couldn't wait to get out, and that was God done with for that term. Back home, of course, I resumed my habitual church attendance with my parents. I was relieved to be back, but quite honestly my heart wasn't in it, because of course God knew exactly what I'd been up to, and couldn't wait to get up to again once I got back to York.

My first (and as it was to turn out my only) year in York was a truly great one, and I still look back on it as one of the highlights of my life so far. Yet it was a year almost totally devoid of God, or at least any overt relationship with him. Reflecting on this time with a mixture of nostalgia and guilt, I discovered another important principle about God's upgrading activities. Some programs on my computer will try to upgrade themselves whether I like it or not, and whether I'm running them or not. But others will only offer me upgrades when I click to start using them. If I haven't used a piece of software for a long time the first thing it will do when I click to run it will be to check for upgrades. During my time in York I wasn't 'running' the God-program at all. On the surface it was not a time of great spiritual insight, wonderful answers to prayer or great strides in sanctification (in fact it was the very opposite). And yet, with hindsight, I think that he was still at work in me, building into me much more self-confidence, healing me from some of the more oppressive aspects of my background and, above all, allowing me to laugh and have fun. By not consciously co-operating with him I think he achieved a lot less than he might have liked, but in the background he was there, and his purposes for me were being worked out. Even as I write this I realise what an outrageous statement the pre-York me would have found this to be: God using my sin and neglect of him for my sanctification. But the more I think about it the more I see what fantastic news this is. You may be having a year (or longer) off God. You may have forgotten or neglected him totally. You may even be enjoying the freedom that that brings. But my experience is that even through the unsanctified behaviour of a bunch of drunken pals God can be at work. Richard Rohr agrees:

> None of us go into our spiritual maturity completely of our own accord, or by a totally free choice. We are led by *Mystery*, which religious people rightly call grace. Most of us have to be cajoled or seduced into it, or we fall into it by some kind of 'transgression', believe it or not; like Jacob finding his birthright through cunning, and Esau losing his by failure.[6]

Apart from God, there was one other small problem: Chemistry. I had done well at A level, but suddenly I discovered I couldn't understand a word anyone was going on about. They might just as well have been teaching me in Chinese. I later heard that this is a well-known phenomenon in science subjects, which is called the 'brick wall' syndrome. So I fell further and further behind, missed more and more deadlines and felt more and more hopeless. And the more hopeless I felt about my work, the more fun I had to try to avoid it.

The crunch was approaching: after Easter we had some preliminary exams, which would give the tutors some idea of how we might do in our Part 1s the following Christmas. Part 1 exams marked the halfway stage through the degree, and provided the crunch point for those who really weren't likely to make it all the way through. Jess and I decided we needed to do some serious revision over the Easter holidays, so we went to the Isle of Man, where his parents had a cottage. Well, you can imagine what happened. I'm not sure either of us opened a book for the entire fortnight, but we had a great holiday. Needless to say I failed my prelims.

'You really do need to buck your ideas up!' my tutor told me. 'If you fail your Part 1s, you're out.' I decided to face reality. 'Statistically speaking, how many people who fail their prelims do get themselves together and carry on successfully?' I asked. 'Hardly any at all,' he replied encouragingly. I asked if I could go away and think about it. I considered the possibility of changing courses and doing Biology instead, but the idea did not really appeal. If I was such a failure at Chemistry, why should another subject be any different? For the next six weeks I did no work at all, went to no lectures or practicals, until eventually the admin office chased me up to see what I had decided to do. By then the decision had been made for me: I was irretrievably behind, and would have no option but to drop out. I still occasionally wake up with nightmares about this period, and am so relieved when I come to and realise that that was all forty-three years ago and I'm OK now.

So, faced with the twin sorrows of leaving my friends (and my new girlfriend) behind and facing the wrath of my parents, I plunged into depression. What on earth was I going to do with my life now? I had decided years ago that teaching was for me, and Chemistry had been my favourite subject at school, but now all that was gone. What was I existing for now? It was into this mood that I heard God speak to me for the first time.

On the campus at York was a Henry Moore sculpture, one of those family groups with holes through their middles. One afternoon I was standing looking at it (I'm not sure why) when I heard God. Not an audible voice, but inside my head the words were as clear as day. I heard him say 'I know you've given up on me, but I haven't given up on you. I still have a plan for your life.' That's it, and it took about as long to happen as it just took you to read those words. Then it was all over, but that brief moment of download gave me just about the greatest upgrade I'd ever had.

First of all, it was a brand new experience to hear God speak at all. Of course there had been lots of sermons about how prayer is meant to be a two-way conversation, and we had to listen as well as present our shopping lists, but no-one had ever modelled it to me or taught me in real terms what that meant. The only prayer I'd ever experienced was strictly a one-way street. So a God who actually communicated was a stunning novelty. Yet I could no more deny what I'd heard than fly to the moon. It was that real.

Then there was what he said. It was so unlike the God I'd been brought up to fear. If he had anything to say to me it would be to tell me to get my act together, stop doing all those naughty student sins and go back to church, or else I'd find myself in the eternal frying-pan. But instead I heard the voice of one who still wanted me, who was sad that I'd neglected him but who still wanted to show me his will so that I could get on with it. And who, although I didn't understand it at the time, was secretly sharpening and polishing me for a purpose even greater than I could have imagined. Nothing could have prepared me for a God of such grace and love. I was completely blown away in the few seconds that encounter took, and my life was literally turned around. I began to seek God afresh, not because I was frightened of his vengeance, but because I was genuinely excited about the possibilities he was holding out before me. I had no idea what they might be, but I still wanted to go with it. This really was the start of an adventure.

Nevertheless it was with a real sense of despair that a few days later I said goodbye to my girlfriend and my mates and headed for Leeds coach station to go home again. I had failed. I was a dropout. I didn't know whether I'd ever see my friends again. I needed God more than ever before.

3

Called to Ministry

It was all very well to set about seeking my new direction in life but I still had to earn some money, so I managed to get a job working for what is now called British Telecom or BT, but which was in those days the Post Office, where my dad was a draughtsman. I worked in the Patents Department, and whenever anyone invented a bit of new telephonic technology I had to search through hundreds of files to find what in that area had already been patented. To be honest I wasn't that taken with it, but it did bring in a few quid. But my real calling lay ahead of me: I wanted to be a musician. I set about scouring the ads in Christian magazines in order to join a band and find my new direction.

I had several abortive auditions: a couple of outfits wanted me but I just didn't like their musical style, and one lot didn't want me because I wasn't musically good enough. At one interview the band said they had a gig that night and invited me to play with them, which I did perfectly competently. But I thought that if the music was so non-taxing that I could just wing it I'd be bored in a few weeks. Indeed I was pretty bored that evening. ELP they weren't!

The breakthrough came when I heard about a guy who was looking to form a band whose musical tastes seemed to match mine and, believe it or not, lived about a mile from my parents' home. We met up, advertised for and found a drummer, and began to rehearse. We were a Hammond organ-based trio, doing stuff that chimed exactly with my Nice/ELP tastes, and in a small way we set Romford alight. But at the end of a year, when the band split up, I was to discover, out of the blue, that I had a calling even greater than playing bass, if that were possible. (The band later reformed with a new line-up, and went on to some fame and fortune. You may have heard of After the Fire if you're old enough.)

Meanwhile I had reconnected with my former Baptist church, and was carrying on trying to be a Christian as though York had never happened. I had also reconnected with some school friends, some of whom had links with other churches locally. One night a friend and I were praying together, when, out of the blue, he told me, 'I think God has given me a prophetic word for you.' Although I believed by now in a God who spoke, I had never really encountered this kind of thing before, so I was all ears but a bit anxious too. 'I think God is calling you to be an Anglican vicar,' he told me, in a way that seemed a bit strange to a struggling Baptist.

Over the years I have become used to people bringing 'words' for others, and my counsel is never to try to make things happen. But in those days that was all I needed. I was off! I knew very little about the Anglican church, except that they were not real Christians and they wore funny robes, so I felt I needed to do a bit of exploration if I was to become a vicar. I set about asking friends whom I knew went to Anglican churches for advice.

I began to attend not one but two very different Anglican churches. The first, St Laurence's, to which a friend's girlfriend invited me, was what you might call 'Anglo-Catholic'. Of course such terms meant nothing to me at that stage, but it basically meant that they had Communion every week, as the main service, rather than once a month tagged on afterwards as we did at the Baptist church. The priests, who were called 'Father', dressed up, there was lots of smoke, and people sang stuff instead of saying it. It seemed a huge distance from any kind of Christianity I'd ever experienced before, and I hated it with such a passion that I had to go back the following week in order to experience the wonderful sense of outrage over again. Soon I found I was hooked. Something in me also appreciated their great patronal festival celebrations. Laurence had been a deacon in a church in Rome somewhere who for a bit of cheek to the Emperor had been martyred in AD 258 by being roasted on a grid over hot coals. So each August the congregation celebrated their patron saint with a great barbecue, which seemed somehow both appropriate and amusing.

St Laurence's was Sunday morning, but Tuesday evenings were very different. Some more friends invited me to another church that was creating a bit of a stir because they had been 'renewed by the Holy Spirit'. The vicar was a guy called Trevor Dearing, and St Paul's, I was later to discover, was one of the early pioneers of a new movement called 'charismatic renewal'. It was a very different experience from my Anglo-Catholic church. For a start you had to get there an hour or so before it started if you wanted a seat. There was no liturgy, and certainly no smoke, but there was plenty of fire, as the Holy Spirit was welcomed to save, baptise, heal and deliver people. The music consisted of short Bible-based 'choruses'; there was usually a period of 'singing in tongues', there was a sermon that called people to be saved, baptised in the Spirit, healed or delivered from evil spirits, and then there was a time for people to go forward and receive prayer. It was crowded, lively, at times noisy and I hated it. In fact I hated it even more than St Laurence's, because apostate though that might have been, at least it wasn't scary. And yet I found myself going back for more. Much later I was to discover a theologian called Rudolph Otto, who talked in a famous book about the *mysterium tremendum et fascinans*, or the 'fascinating but terrifying mystery' of God.[7] There is something about him, said Otto, which scares the wits out of us but keeps us coming back for more. That was certainly true of me at this period in my life.

Gradually I began to relax into both manifestations of Anglicanism. I came to appreciate the fine music and dignified liturgy of St Laurence's and, while I still hated it, I came gradually to realise that what I was seeing at St Paul's was much more like authentic New Testament Christianity than anything I had experienced before. It occurred to me that, noisy though the ministry times might be – particularly if there was any deliverance from evil spirits going on, I could keep my distance. No-one was going to force anything on me that I wasn't ready for.

Most intriguing was all this stuff about 'baptism in the Spirit'. As I've already said, during my Christian upbringing the Spirit was hardly ever mentioned. I can remember attending a friend's Bible study group where they talked about the 'gifts of the Spirit', concluding quite quickly and without controversy that they were not for today. I certainly hadn't ever seen any, not that I knew what they were anyway, so I was quite happy with this outcome. But other friends thought differently. They were beginning to speak of experiences of the Spirit that meant that they had started 'speaking in tongues', a rather weird activity that I was familiar with from St Paul's but that seemed crazy to me. I discovered a kind of secret subculture of people who, due to persecution from their churches, felt they had to keep quiet about their experiences, but could no more deny them than they could deny their Lord. There was a kind of naughty fascination about this time, which coupled with my gradual intellectual acceptance of the work of the Spirit, was reshaping my understanding of Christian life.

One night at St Paul's I could stand it no longer. My resistance had been eroded away, and before I realised what was happening I found myself down at the front, kneeling at the Communion rail, and waiting to be 'baptised in the Spirit'. The clergy ministering came inexorably closer along the rail: the girl before me, when hands were laid on her head, burst immediately into floods of tears and a torrent of tongues, and then it was me. I felt the hands on my head . . . and that was all I felt. Absolutely nothing happened. No great feelings, no new closeness to God, certainly no spiritual gifts. Zilch. I got up and went back to my seat, greatly relieved and terribly disappointed.

For the next two years I continued as an intellectually convinced but experientially untouched charismatic. Various friends tried different theological explanations on me. I had to believe that I had in fact been baptised in the Spirit, even though there was aboslutely no evidence.

'The evidence will follow your faith,' I was told.

'Not everyone gets the gift of tongues' – which had become for me the great acid test of my charismatic status.

'Did you dabble in the occult or take LSD while you were at unversity?' No to both.

'Sometimes it's better to think of the "release" of the Spirit rather than the "baptism" of the Spirit. It isn't that you haven't received the Spirit, but that his work in you hasn't been released into the outside world.'

None of these explanations really seemed to help: I still felt inferior, not quite the charismatic ticket, and convinced that some secret sin was holding me back. Could it have been, for example, that Rabbentaft was actually an occult practice?

All these difficulties were swept away at a stroke, though, the night I did begin to speak in tongues. I was in a B&B at Whitesands Bay in Pembrokeshire, and I can still remember those awful nylon sheets that caught in your toenails every time you tried to turn over. At last I had joined the club: I was a proper charismatic!

My journey towards vicaring, though, was progressing more slowly. Much as I had come to feel warily at home in both my Anglican churches, I couldn't really feel that my future lay in either of these directions. Another friend helped me out by suggesting that I might like to try a third church; St Luke's. They were Anglican, without a doubt, so I would be able to fulfil my friend's prophetic word there, but they had neither the liturgical excesses of St Laurence's nor the noisy extravagances of St Paul's. She was sure the vicar there would be only too glad to help me on my way to ordination.

So I can remember knocking on the vicarage door one evening. 'You don't know me,' I told the very tall man who answered the door, 'but God is calling me to the Anglican ministry. What do I have to do?'

John was very gracious, although, I can now understand, a bit wary too. He invited me to worship with them, and told me that the first step would need to be confirmation, a ceremony about which I knew absolutely nothing. I began to attend St Luke's, and found it to be doctrinally not that different from my Baptist upbringing, but a lot more gracious. They took the Bible seriously, didn't go mad on the liturgy and, although John told me that he was one of these new 'charismatics', the church had not yet experienced the outrageous behaviour of St Paul's (that was to come later). Eventually I joined the confirmation group, and formally severed my ties with the Baptist church of my youth. One friend was particularly concerned at this step, because, as he told me, 'Anglicans don't worship God; they worship a golden dog,' a mark of the ecumenical ignorance of the times.

I had a bit of a tussle over the confirmation bit, though. I went obediently to the classes, but could simply not see the need for it. I had been baptised (my Baptist baptism by total immersion apparently had worked) and I had by now received the Holy Spirit, so why on earth did I need to go through yet another ceremony? The vicar's answer was very pragmatic: because if you don't you can't get ordained. I struggled with this for weeks, until one day I was struck by the story of Jesus' baptism. He asked John the Baptist to put him through what was for him a completely needless and meaningless ceremony, since John's baptism was about repentance for sins, and Jesus was by definition sinless. But his reply to John's protestations was basically 'Just do it: if those are the rules, I'm happy to go through with it, whether I need it or not' (at least that's how I translated 'it is proper for us to do this to fulfil all right-eousness', Matt. 3:15). And in fact when he did go through his meaningless ceremony just to keep the rules, it was the occasion for a major blessing as the Father ripped heaven apart, anointed him with the Holy Spirit, and declared his love and favour for all to hear. Similarly my confirmation, far from being meaningless, was a time for me of significant meeting with God.

The road to ordination in the Anglican church can be a long one, with a series of interviews with scary members of the hierarchy, culminating in what is now called a BAP (Bishop's Advisory Panel) but was then called an ACCM (Advisory Council on the Church's Ministry or something like that). This is a residential conference consisting of a series of inter-views, observed group discussions and worship. By now I had found a more permanent job working in manufactur-ing pharmacy, but when a vacancy came up in the delivery section I applied for that and got it. I was now delivering surgical instruments to hospitals, and being interviewed for my future ministry in my spare time. Finally, after four years, I was sent to my ACCM. I was not selected.

This was a bit of a blow to say the least. The reasons given were that I had only recently joined the C of E (and a somewhat suspect bit of it at that), so I needed more time to get used to her funny ways. At least it was a 'not yet' verdict rather than 'Not on your nelly, ever'. My Diocesan Director of Ordinands, the senior clergyman whose job was to look after me and steer me through the process, asked me what I thought I might do now. I decided that I would like to go and do a theology degree anyway, so that if I was selected later I'd already be some way along the training process, and if I wasn't at least I would have redeemed my York dropout status.

In those days we got student grants, rather than loans, but I'd already had one, if only for my first year, so I would have to finance myself for a year. I tried to find ways around this, but there was nothing anyone could do. This was a major disaster, since the only way that I could afford to train would be to live at home with my parents, and the only college within reach was King's in the Strand in London. And all good evangelicals in the 1970s knew that King's was the lair of Satan himself. I was told by many friends how they would set out to destroy my faith, how no-one emerged still believing anything, how the tutors were all atheists and so on. I would quite likely end up gay into the bargain. How would I possibly survive?

Terrifying though these prospects were I simply had no option, other than to continue working for a few more years and save up to go away to a safer college. Thus with great trepidation I enrolled at King's for a Theology BD course. My friends at home prayed fervently for me as I entered this nether world of darkness.

Much against my expectations I found very quickly that I loved it at King's. The tutors were largely friendly and helpful, many of them were saintly and deeply pastoral, and the theology I was starting to learn was gripping. I quickly made some great friends and, although our exploits were not quite as silly as those of our gang in York, we nevertheless had some tremendous student fun. We all had to do Greek, but because I wanted to specialise in Old Testament I had to learn Hebrew too. Our Hebrew tutor was friendly, kind and fun, while the Greek tutor was from the old school and educated us by sarcasm and humiliation. If you knew you might be picked at random from the class to stand up and recite some verb endings or do a piece of unseen translation, you did the work in advance, believe me! It's not at all fashionable nowadays to educate people through fear, but it worked for me. My Hebrew was never as good as my Greek, something that I regret to this day.

I also learnt the truth of the maxim, 'education is too precious to be wasted on the young'. As a 'mature' student (well, working on it, anyway) I worked hard and diligently, handed my essays in on time and generally achieved pretty good marks. I had enjoyed York for the social life, but now I was here to work and learn.

As for the 'liberal' theology for which King's at that time was renowned, I needn't have worried. I found the lecturers fair and even-handed, balancing different opinions by different scholars and leaving us to make up our own minds. They were less bothered about what we believed as long as we could argue our case convincingly. I had seen the world of academic theology as a faith-destroying threat: in fact I realised that it genuinely was a search for truth. If some of my tutors didn't believe in the demonic world, or the gifts of the Spirit, it was simply because they had not yet encountered such things, and that like all of us they were children of their own cultures. If you start from the modernist presupposition that the supernatural cannot possibly exist, of course you have to do some clever work on the text of a Bible that seems to believe that it does. But the work they did was honest, and had integrity given the presuppositions on which they based it. To work with different presuppositions would lead to different conclusions, but the important thing as far as they were concerned was that the work was thorough and fair. I don't think any of us in the minority evangelical constituency ever felt undermined or attacked for our beliefs, although we were made to ask some hard questions about them.

As the course went on we had to decide on some specialist papers to take and some options to concentrate less on. I dropped Ethics and Church History like they were hot bricks, and focused instead on Old Testament and Liturgy – subjects for which I retain a great love to this day. It would be fair to say that these were both something of minority subjects; Old Testament because of the need to learn Hebrew, and Liturgy because – it's a minority subject. So there was quite a bit of camaraderie amongst those of us who chose them. I remember when the entire group was invited to Sunday lunch by one of our lecturers, along with all the staff of the Old Testament department. In that room were some of the greatest brains in Old Testament scholarship in the country: Peter Ackroyd, Richard Coggins, Ulrich Simon, Michael Knibb, as well as a few aspiring students. So imagine our delight to discover that earlier that morning a leaflet had been pushed through the door from some quasi-Christian sect about how Old Testament prophesies proved that the

end of the world was due on some date or other, and that
someone would be calling later in the day to discuss it with
us. I could just imagine the delight of some poor door-to-
door knocker finding he had stumbled upon a room full of
academic Old Testament scholars, most of whom didn't even
believe in the end of the world, let alone the Old Testament
proving it, but sadly the second coming was delayed and the
promised return never did happen. That would have been
such fun to watch!

The other thing God downloaded into my life at this stage was
a wife. I'd met Chris through a friend, and at the start of our
relationship I was most definitely on the rebound, having just
emerged from a long relationship with my previous girlfriend.
Chris was a member of the church I eventually landed up in,
but was away at college. We started going out in the Easter
holidays, during a parish weekend at church led by the Fisher-
folk, a group of charismatic Christians with a ministry of faith
sharing, but we were warned off by our curate who told us that
we had to leave a three-month gap between my break-up with
Caroline and the start of a new relationship. So we conducted
a clandestine relationship for three months, before going
public. In fact I realised after two weeks that Chris was the
one for me, and I sort of proposed at Kew Gardens. But it
had to be a long-distance relationship for a while, as Chris
was in the second year of a four-year course in Dudley in the
West Midlands. Eventually we were married on Christmas Eve
1977. I just couldn't understand why our parish clergy tried
to put us off that day, claiming that it was a busy enough time
for them without weddings as well! I can now. We had not one

but two honeymoons, in Bath and Portugal, and Chris went back to her teaching job and I went back to college.

In my final year I went back to ACCM, and this time I passed with flying colours. Having done a purely academic degree I now had to spend a year at another college for some more practical and pastoral training. I chose Durham, making the decision before I'd even got off the train. As you come into the station the railway line bends and suddenly a panoramic view of the city opens up before you. I knew instantly that this was where I wanted to be!

I had enjoyed my studies so much that I wanted more, so as well as my practical training I signed on to do a masters' degree. I find that many clergy are a bit ambivalent about the academic nature of theological training, but I have never had those kinds of doubts. I had lived with my faith since my earliest years, but I was now having the chance to engage my brain as well. My head was catching up with my heart and, rather than feeling a division or tension between the two, I found that they complemented each other perfectly. In another upgrade God was putting into me a love of learning and study, and the realisation that true Christian faith does not require that one leaves one's brain in the umbrella stand by the door. I think also at this stage that God was giving me some of the skills that would come to the fore later as a teacher, and in particular the ability to make quite complicated subjects accessible to those without PhDs. One of the most common comments on my preaching and teaching since then has been that I help people to understand God better, and that I help them to think more deeply. This is a gift for which I am profoundly grateful. I don't consider myself a heavyweight academic, but I really value thinking about my faith, and I really value the ability to help others to do so too.

Our time in the beautiful city of Durham passed quickly, but before it came to an end God was to do perhaps the most profound and painful of his works in me. Little did I know what was coming.

$-4-$

Breakdown

It was a Monday lunchtime in January. I was in the college dining room, just finishing my meal, when suddenly and without any warning the whole room started to spin. I felt sick and terrified, and knew I just had to get out of there. Clutching the pillars I made it to the door, down the corridor and out into the street where, clinging onto walls and lampposts like a Saturday night clubber, I finally managed the walk home. The world had just about stopped spinning, but the sense of fear had not subsided. I wondered what on earth was happening to me. I'd never experienced anything like this before.

Eventually I made it to my GP's surgery. He explained that I had had a panic attack, and prescribed some valium. He didn't seem all that bothered. But for the next few months I was barely able to get out of bed, living with a sense of fear and dread all the time that occasionally rose to a crescendo of blind panic. I felt unable to talk to anyone about what was going on for me, since the only way I had to describe my symptoms was that I was 'going mad'. I found it impossible to be in college, or any other public place, since I feared that a panic attack would hit me and that I would start screaming and have to run from the room, making a public exhibition of myself. And of course I was terrified of taking the valium, since that would prove beyond belief that I had 'gone mental' and in any case I might become addicted. I still have most of the tablets today. They may well be past their expiry date, come to think of it.

Chris was kind and sympathetic but bewildered at what had happened to her husband. She was working full time, and most evenings came in to find me lying on the sofa just as she had left me in the morning. I lived with this pain for the next five years, although very gradually it either abated or I got used to it. Some days I could feel it physically, like a tight band around my head, but at other times it was more like a dull mental ache, if that makes any sense.

The first person with whom I was able to share what was going on for me was John, my best mate at college. He was a Glaswegian with an incredible sense of fun and humour (who was tragically killed in a car accident in Berlin a few years after his ordination). I can't now remember how the conversation started, but it turned out that he too had suffered from this kind of illness, which he described as 'a bit of trouble with my nerves'. This was a phrase I had heard a few times, but for the first time understood what it meant. He was able to describe my feelings back to me, which reassured me that I was not the first person in the history of the universe to have experienced symptoms like this. Secondly, he was able, with his superior knowledge and background in nursing, to reassure me that I wasn't going mad. Whatever the term 'mad' actually means, it has no relationship with the panic attacks that I was experiencing, other than being another kind of mental illness. To worry about 'going mad' as a result of panic attacks is like worrying that your leg will drop off if you have toothache: it's just a completely different illness.

I found this information immensely reassuring, but my symptoms persisted. That June I managed to survive being ordained in Norwich Cathedral (I think I may have given in and popped a valium that day), and moved to begin my first curacy in a Norfolk market town. I had learnt by now to cope with the mental pain, and accepted that it did not inevitably lead to symptoms of blind panic. In fact the acute episodes were pretty few and far between, although of course there was the perpetual fear that one would come and hit me from nowhere. But most of the time I lived with what I had by now discovered were called 'free-floating anxiety states'.

I began to keep a kind of graph on which I rated each day as a '3' day – really bad anxiety, '2', '1' or the theoretical '0' days – no pain of any kind. Over the months I discovered two things: that the number of '3' days decreased and the number of '2' and '1' days slowly increased, and that when I did have a '3' day I could usually identify a cause. It was often a deadline, or another particularly stressful occasion.

By now, as you can imagine, I had developed a certain morbid interest in the world of mental health and psychotherapy, and on arrival in Norfolk I did two things: I found myself a therapist, and signed up for a year's course of evening counselling classes at Norwich City College. I discovered that Norwich had a huge counselling and therapy 'scene', and I found our group sessions, which were a mixture of theoretical teaching and experiential working, an absolute lifeline. We were a disparate group of people, but I found there a community of acceptance and healing that was exactly what I needed. We explored many different models of counselling, as well as the basic skills that were essential across the board, and I found myself to be something of a natural.[8] I had some curiosity value as an Anglican clergyman, but this assorted bunch of New Agers, hypnotists and occultists, who populated the strange fringes of the Norwich therapy scene, accepted me. I was even invited to celebrate a Eucharist at our weekend residential after I had been priested at my second ordination.

One member of the group was of particular help to me. Like my friend at college, Anne had herself suffered from the same things, and was able once again to describe what I was going through with the insights that only a fellow sufferer could have gained. It had been several years ago for her and, of course, I was anxious above all else to know how all this was going to end. I'll never forget her words, which brought tears of relief to my eyes: 'You *will* get better!'

My personal therapist was a lot less eclectic than our evening class: he was a Gestaltist, and I quickly developed an immense respect and liking for what is considered by many to be a somewhat strange, on-the-fringe method of therapy.[9] We had had a session or two looking at Gestalt on the course, but to work week by week with a proper thera-pist was both fascinating and immensely healing. Eventually. But in the meantime I found it, as well as fascinating, to be pretty frustrating, and therein, I believe, was my salvation, my upgrade from God.

Peter was a Christian, and shared my faith and some of the questions that my illness had raised for me. But, being a Gestalt therapist, he had a different approach. Rather than trying to answer my agonised theological questions, he would suddenly say, 'Your leg moved while you were saying that! If your leg had a voice, what would it want to say?'

This isn't the place for a full exposition of the philosophy and methodology of Gestalt therapy, but it is basically about integration, completing the whole. Where there are gaps our words, thoughts, dreams and bodies will try to tell us so that we can pay attention and gain the insight we need to close the gaps and thus attain insight and wholeness. Sounds weird, I know. Just the kind of stuff therapists talk about. But for me it gradually became a life-saver.

The thing is, I wanted answers. I wanted to understand. But Peter wanted to stop me getting any answers, and teach me to learn to live with the uncertainty. I remember on one occasion he led me, as Gestalt therapists often do, on a 'fantasy journey' or what we might call a guided meditation. In my imagination I saw the top of my head sliced off, and a spring with a ball at the end pop out and start rotating. Something like that, anyway. I can remember when I 'woke up' being filled with questions: Why had my head split in half? Why a ball on a spring? Why was it rotating *anti*-clock-wise? Above all, what did it all *mean*? Peter was at his most frustrating that day: he just kept asking me back how it had felt to have my head lose its lid. The more I asked questions, the more he simply said, 'I've no idea!' How was this going to get me better?

But what emerged over the months, and this is why I believe that Gestalt therapy was exactly the right model for me, was a realisation that my whole life, and my whole faith, had been about a quest for certainty. I had been brought up,

as you have heard, in the kind of church where being 'right' –
or, as we put it, 'sound' – was the only thing which counted.
We even used to sing that old song:

  I'm S-O-U-N-D
  I'm S-O-U-N-D
  I know I am, I'm sure I am!
  I'm S-O-U-N-D

Someone once said, a bit unkindly perhaps, that evangelical-
ism isn't a theological position; it's a neurosis. Overstated of
course, but I came gradually to see that there could be some
truth in it, and that the preoccupation in some bits of the
church with correct doctrine and the witch hunting of those
who disagreed was not perhaps the most healthy of lifestyles
to have pursued. I came to understand that studying theology
at one of the most 'liberal' places in the country had set up a
huge dichotomy within me. I had loved every minute of my
theological education, and had come to value, while not always
swallowing whole, the insights of critical theological study.
But deep within me the desire always to get it right was still
lurking. As I approached the end of my training, and was about
to be ordained and launched into a waiting world, this tension
became acute. I came to understand that it was significant that
my initial 'breakdown' on that fateful Monday morning came
immediately after a visit to my potential first parish, during
which the deal had been done and I had agreed to go there.

So to use my therapy session to understand what was going
on for me, to explain my symptoms and to tie them down

exactly to different kinds of stress-inducing events was merely playing into my weakness. Peter's refusal to join in with that game, his repeated answers of 'I've no idea!' to my agonised questions, gradually taught me that it might be easier all round if I just stopped asking silly questions and accepted the fact that life was messy and things happened. And in terms of my faith, I came painfully and slowly to realise that God doesn't always have to explain himself to me, and that now and again he might just do things that I don't understand, and that I don't need to understand.

It was also Peter who, in one of our very early sessions, responded to my use of the term 'breakdown' with the simple question 'Breakdown, or breakthrough?' I came to understand, and I guess this is a huge part of my motivation in writing this now, that to some extent we have a choice. When life crumbles around us do we simply cave in, or do we seek to move into a new way of living and understanding? Do we accept and download, or simply try to live on with the bug-infested old version of ourselves?

This journey away from certainty is one that has been well documented in other places, particularly in the work of sociologists such as Fowler and Westerhoff[10] who have researched faith development. While the schemes of these two scholars are different in some respects, they share an understanding that the childlike (or even childish) simplicity has to take account, as we grow up, of the realities of life where prayers do not always get answered instantly, in spite of the Bible's apparent assurance that they will. We need to cope, as indeed the biblical writers had to, with the problems of innocent suffering, the apparent victory of evildoers, the certainty of death and all the other hard questions that adult life throws at us. The certainties of the early years of faith have to give way to something much broader, something far less certain of its own truths and neat little schemes, and ultimately to the ability to realise that until we meet our Father face to face there will be all sorts of things that we simply have no way of understanding. And then, of course, there is the equally difficult task of deciding what we *can* be certain about. One criticism of Fowler's work has been that he is suggesting that Christians are not fully mature until they have become liberals and let go of any semblance of orthodox faith.

I find some of Job's agonised cries really inspiring: 'Though he slay me, yet will I hope in him' (Job 13:15) and 'I know that my redeemer lives, and that in the end he will stand on the earth' (Job 19:25). The art of understanding that we can't understand what is going on, but that we can trust the one behind it, is a difficult thing to achieve, but an essential one for Christian maturity.

So very gradually my Gestalt work was turning my breakdown into a breakthrough, as I learnt to relax into the experience of not knowing rather than seeking desperately to get all my ducks lined up. As I did so I found that this skill was transferable to my symptoms. Someone had said in the early days that I should regard my panic attacks as welcome friends, a suggestion that seemed both laughable and cruel. But now I was able, in true Gestalt style, simply to *experience* the attacks, knowing that they would soon pass, and would not overwhelm me in the way I had previously feared.

I did not totally abandon my quest for understanding. I have always been the kind of person who likes to get my head around things, usually in order that I might explain them helpfully to others. As the acuteness of my symptoms diminished, I became interested in studying them with a kind of academic detachment, seeking to understand what was going on, but not as though my life or sanity depended on it. I signed on for a second year of counselling training, and began to research mental illness in general and anxiety states in particular. I discovered that around 25 per cent of the population will at some time or another experience acute anxiety or panic attacks. I found out the kind of people who were most likely to suffer, and the sorts of triggers that could set off attacks. I found out that for some people, like me, the big fear was of 'going mad', while for others the symptoms felt like they imagined a heart attack would feel, so that they decided they were in fact about to die, a fate that made merely screaming and running from the room seem like a much more positive alternative.

I understood more of the biochemistry involved, and that a panic attack is basically an adrenaline overdose. I realised that the glands responsible for producing adrenaline could only work at that capacity for a few seconds, and that the acute phase would never last very long at all – although after the primary fear that triggers the attack there is then secondary fear, which is the fear of another attack. I learnt that simple procedures like deliberate deep breathing could help reduce stress levels, and I discovered 'biofeedback' – the use of a device to measure changes in the skin's electrical conductance and translate them into an audible signal.

This allows you literally to hear your mounting anxiety when an attack is coming, and act through deliberate relaxation to weaken or even stop it before it hits. I'm not a doctor, but this kind of information served to rob my symptoms of much of their dread and, over the years, as I have explained it to other sufferers, I have seen the relief on their faces as some kind of basic insight has been discovered. I also gained quite a bit of perspective when I realised that, painful though the experience had been, anxiety is pretty far down the list of severity of mental illnesses. Many, many people suffer symptoms considerably worse than anything I experienced.

It was about five years before Anne's promise to me came completely true, and I gave up plotting my graph – as pretty much every day was a '0' day. All that was nearly thirty years ago now, and on only a handful of occasions have my symptoms returned. They have never really taken hold, and I have always been able to identify the particular stresses that have brought them on. But if you were to ask me if I would go through it all again if I had the choice, I would find that really hard to answer. I know that God downloaded into me a much more mature, and paradoxically less certain, faith – at least a lot less certain about the things we simply can't be certain about. But at the same time my faith in God is so much stronger, I would say well balanced, and helpful to others. I do not consider myself to have taken leave of orthodox Christian beliefs, but I do have a very much more well-developed awareness that I might not actually be right 100 per cent of the time. All in all I think it was probably worth it.

If you have been affected by any of the issues raised in this chapter, there is a particularly helpful section on the Mind website: http://www.mind.org.uk/mental_health_a-z/8001_anxiety_and_panic_attacks. This not only describes the kinds of symptoms you might be experiencing, but also suggests some strategies for getting over them.

And my friend Anne would say to you, 'You *will* get better.'

5

Doing the Stuff

It was now 1984, and after three years in parish ministry I was beginning to feel that I knew what I was doing. My anxiety symptoms had receded to the point where I was able to lead a pretty normal life, and I was enjoying parish ministry. Our first son Steve had been born two years earlier, although only just. Poor Chris spent twenty-three hours in labour, during which she was taken on a mad blue-light dash from our local cottage hospital to the Norfolk and Norwich, complete with torrential storms that meant that even the ambulance had to pull over for a while until things abated and the driver could see where he was going. That whole experience scarred me for life: I still have to look away when anyone on the telly is giving birth. How I managed to survive it twice more I shall never know. Paul was born nineteen months later, and this time we told them we'd go straight into Norwich, if they didn't mind. In fact his birth was about as OK as births can be from the point of view of the father standing helplessly by.

So we lived as a little family, and the boys became firm friends as well as brothers, as they still are today, even though their lives have taken very different courses. The experience of being a dad was terrifying, but gave me a whole new understanding of God as my father, which corrected some of the lingering misapprehensions from my own spiritual upbringing.

As the boys began to grow up, another one of those chance things dropped into our lives began to come to fruition. Long before we were married we had heard a guy called Barry Kissell, who was attached to St Andrew's Church in Chorleywood, talking about his own children, and how at the age of 5 they knew enough about their faith to be praying for and evangelising their friends. They knew that not everybody believed what they believed, but that the love of Jesus was for all. They were also able to give a defence of the hope they had. At the time, having not really thought about children ourselves, we were impressed, but as soon as we had some of our own God downloaded into us the truth of that talk, and we were determined from day one that we would not 'leave them to make up their own minds' but would rather bring them up to become mature Christians in their own right. We have since come to believe, and have written about it too, that this is the prime task of Christian parents, and it breaks our hearts to see how deeply some people have bought into the politically correct agenda of not trying to 'proselytise' our children, or of expecting the church to do our work of nurture for us. Having understood this it seemed the most appropriate thing in the world to have them baptised, and the final piece of my Baptist scruples fell away completely.[11]

So life was good, but something was missing. I was due another upgrade.

At first I couldn't quite put my finger on what I was feeling. But at Easter 1984 we went, as was our custom, to Spring

Harvest, our Christian festival of choice. It was one of those weeks when every single speaker said the same thing. I went to a whole variety of seminars, celebrations and workshops, but I could only hear one message: it's no good just telling people about God if we don't help them to experience God in action. I realised that this had neatly articulated my dilemma: although we were seeing gradual evangelism and church growth, it all seemed a bit tame and powerless. I wanted more of God. I'd spent long enough believing in him by faith: I wanted to see some raw power.

While Spring Harvest had helped me articulate the question, it did nothing to provide me with any answers. But a month or so later I read an article in the magazine of Anglican Renewal Ministries (a magazine that I was later to edit, little did I know) about the visit of David Watson, a charismatic church leader from York, to an American church leader in Los Angeles called John Wimber. The article described the remarkable ministry that John's church in Anaheim had of healing, deliverance and supernatural evangelism. I knew I had to get some of this, and fortunately I wouldn't have to cross the Atlantic to get it. John was to visit Holy Trinity Brompton (HTB), a large Anglican church in West London, to run a taster day in preparation for a full conference in November. I booked my place instantly.

A couple of us left Norwich at 4 a.m. to get a coach to Victoria, and finally arrived home at 2 a.m. the next day. That day changed my life. John was a loveable man, an engaging teacher, a great wit and a not half bad musician. In the course of a few hours teaching and practicals he taught us how to invite the Holy Spirit to come and engage with people, how to spot the physical signs of his presence and how we might go on to pray for people. He taught us about 'words of knowledge', one of the gifts of the Spirit mentioned in 1 Corinthians 12, whereby we could listen to God and gain information about people in the congregation and what prayer needs they might have, in order to encourage them to come forward for prayer. And we saw all kinds of things happening, the like of which I'd never seen before, at least not in such concentrated form.

But it wasn't actually the ministry times that I found most enthralling; it was the teaching. I had been taught at King's by a bunch of tutors and professors that included amongst them avowed atheists, and others of whom had a faith that was unrecognisable to a keen young evangelical like me. I arrived at King's believing that I didn't really need to do all that clever academic stuff, because I knew Jesus. I knew beyond doubt that he existed, and I knew exactly what his message was: he preached a Pauline gospel of justification by grace through faith. But my tutors seemed to have a different idea. They taught me that Jesus preached about the 'Kingdom of God'. This world was ruled by the devil, but in Jesus God had broken in to defeat the devil and to undo all his evil works. Jesus taught about the values of the Kingdom, told stories about what it was like and then demonstrated it by reversing all the nasty things that entered our world, bringing healing, forgiveness, deliverance and all the rest. One day Jesus would return, so the Bible seemed to teach, and the Kingdom would come in all its fullness. Evil wouldn't just be defeated; it would be destroyed. Of course no-one believed that Jesus actually did heal anyone, or that the devil really existed, or that Jesus would return, but in the primitive worldview of first-century Palestine that's what they would have *believed* Jesus was up to. It was all symbolic, of course: a slightly naïve way of talking about the time when all humankind would live in peace and harmony and walk hand in hand off into the sunset, and all that other liberal stuff.

As I had listened to my lectures at King's I had had to admit that the text of Scripture did actually talk about the Kingdom quite a bit. How had I missed it before? Poor old Paul hardly got a look in: Jesus was all about a Kingdom that had broken in but had not yet come fully. The more I heard, the more it made sense, although as one stubbornly holding on to the belief that Jesus did actually heal and would return I had a bit of a dilemma that completely passed by my more 'Enlightenment' chums. At the end of three years I could write a mean essay on the Kingdom of God. But I never really thought to ask the obvious question.

Now fast forward eight years, and there I was sitting in a church in London hearing the cuddly American telling me exactly the same things I'd heard at King's. But this time there was a difference: once the teaching was finished we got on and did the stuff we'd been learning about. Every bell within my head started to ring as I saw before my eyes the reality of all that great theology. I was hooked, not because I liked it particularly (some of it was a bit scary, if I'm honest) but because I knew in my head that this was right.

A few years later I heard a talk by one of John's Vineyard leaders who was no mean theologian himself, a guy called Don Williams. He claimed that 'Third Wave' ministry (as it came to be called) was the fulfilment of the very best in biblical theology. He traced the thinking of some of the greatest theologians of the twentieth century, most of whom I had studied at King's, and showed how their work was brilliant, biblical and accurate. 'But not one of them,' he continued, 'ever thought to stop and ask the question "So where is it?"' In the Third Wave we're seeing all this brilliant theology worked out before our very eyes. As with my early encounters with charismatic renewal, I was convinced intellectually before I bought it all emotionally.

Later that year I went to the first major 'Signs and Wonders' conference at Westminster Central Hall, which was the 'main course' for which the day at HTB had been the 'starter'. We were able to hear much more detailed teaching, and take part in many more ministry times. More than ever I was convinced, and was determined to go back to Norfolk and give it all a go. John had told us during the week that, in his experience, it took nearly a year of praying and inviting the Spirit before you actually saw any healings, so the following Sunday evening I decided we'd go for it, on the basis that the sooner we started the sooner the year would be over and we'd see something happening. So that first evening my faith levels were zero as we listened to God, as we'd been taught, for words of knowledge. It was all about obedience, not faith.

We got eleven words for people, eleven people responded and, as we prayed, all of them experienced some degree of healing. I don't know why I was better at it than John Wimber, but we were flying! From then on we began to offer prayer ministry whenever we could. Over the next few years I absorbed all I could from John and his team, attending conferences all over the show, and even having the privilege of spending a fortnight at John's church in California. I began to teach the stuff myself, and, working with a team from our small Norfolk church, and later from a much larger church in Sheffield, I developed something of a travelling ministry as a purveyor of Wimberism.

One of the more dubious fruits of John's ministry came from a visit to our church in Sheffield by John and some of his team following a conference in 1985. At one evening meeting, on 5 November as it happens, there was a prophetic word from God about young people being anointed for 'power evangelism'. At the same time the vicar, Robert Warren, felt God speaking to him and telling him that he was about to add several hundred young people to the church. That night the ill-fated 'Nine O'Clock Service' was conceived as the Spirit fell upon many young people from the church in a scene that resembled the aftermath of a major train disaster. History tells the story of NOS, and it is a sad story about how even the best and most God-inspired things can go pear-shaped. But I have no doubt that its origins were sound, and born out of a move of God and a real desire to see young people find healing and salvation for broken lives. It's just that human character and its defects, and human choices, can so easily get in the way. In fact, as John's studies demonstrated, history is littered with tragic stories of moves of God going wrong when fallible humans get their hands on them.[12]

John Wimber died in 1997, and since then many have tried to evaluate and critique his ministry and theological emphases. The Vineyard 'denomination' (John would have rejected this term) continues to thrive in many areas of the world, and his emphasis on the supernatural ministry of all Christians, even if somewhat overstated, provided a powerful upgrade for the evangelical church. Above all the Kingdom theology, which I had been taught so thoroughly at King's but had totally missed until John demonstrated it, provides what I believe is the most helpful explanation for unanswered prayer. To be honest I have wavered in my commitment to healing prayer ministry: I have seen some undoubted miracles, but nowhere near as many as I would have liked to have seen – and I have also taken quite a few funerals.

I look back on this phase of my Christian experience with great fondness, and also a degree of wistfulness. But there was a lot more fun to come yet!

We left Sheffield in 1989 (more of that later) and went to live, somewhat reluctantly, in Coventry, where, after eight years of curacy, I was to be the boss. I had never expected the culture shock of moving from being a curate to becoming the vicar to be that much of an issue, but in fact I found it much harder than the jump from college to curacy. We had been invited to a 'dedication service' for a new baby in South London, and I had managed to get a rare Sunday off, so we got up early and drove off for the day. As a liturgist I can't help but evaluate acts of worship: I try to concentrate on God and simply worship him, in spite of how I'm being led from the front, but I just can't do it. I have to say this particular one was a disaster! I sat there feeling more and more miserable at the bad theology, dreadful music and inept leadership. Above all I felt cheated out of a Sunday off, a chance to be led in worship rather than being up front myself.

As we were driving home that evening through central London, we talked about how sad we felt, and how we wished we could go to a good church. That was when we had the idea of going to the evening service at HTB in Kensington, the same church where I had first heard John Wimber. We diverted from our homeward route, and arrived in plenty of time in the Brompton Road. It wasn't easy to find somewhere to park: there seemed to be a lot more cars around than I'd experienced there before, but eventually we tucked in and walked to the church, only to find huge queues waiting to get in. I knew it was a famous church, but this was just silly!

Finally we got some seats on the balcony, and the service began. The vicar greeted us, and told us that, 'We are living in times of an extraordinary outpouring of God's Spirit!' Oh dear. More charismatic hype.

He then went on to tell us about the visit of a member of his team to a Vineyard church near Toronto Airport. Apparently they were experiencing some incredible manifestations of the Holy Spirit. She had come back and spoken at a staff meeting about what had been going on, at which point the Spirit began to do exactly the same things to the assembled company. That had been ten days ago, and so significant was this move of the Spirit felt to be that it had taken over the agenda of the church. The rest is history, and whatever you think of the so-called 'Toronto Blessing' we were there, completely by 'chance', right at the start of it. There did seem to be something 'catching' about it, because we returned to Coventry only to see an outbreak of the same kinds of phenomena there, not just in our own church but in another that had come into contact with the 'Blessing' by a different

route, but at the same time. Quickly, many more churches in
the city became involved.

One of the features of churches touched by this move
seemed to be continual meetings, and so my church in
Coventry put on a fortnight of evening sessions, where, in
true Vineyard style, we would worship (by which we meant
singing songs), hear some biblical teaching and then invite
the Spirit to come and do what he wanted to do. I remember
these times as times of great blessing, but above all, tremendous fun. And I remember particularly our children and
teenagers being involved up to the hilt, playing or singing
in the worship band, ministering and being ministered to.
Virtually all of the youngsters who were involved with us at
that stage have stayed faithful to God, and many are now
serving him in various capacities and in various parts of the
world. I can't help but believe that seeing God in action
so powerfully is a major factor in avoiding the drop-off of
teenagers from the church that has become almost expected
in many circles.[13]

Two years later I had a sabbatical and we were able to visit
not just the Toronto Airport church (which by then had
severed its links with the Vineyard movement) but also the
'revival' at a Pentecostal church in Brownsville, Pensacola,
which was hitting the Christian headlines at the time. My
conclusion was that we had seen pretty much the same move
of God, but that it had been wrapped up in very different
cultures. At HTB the Spirit had moved in a gentle, Anglican kind of style, with nothing *too* outrageous and a sense of
quiet dignity. In Toronto it had been laid-back Vineyardy in
its feel, and at Pensacola it had been full-on in-yer-face noisy

southern Pentecostal. I knew which I preferred, but I was amazed at the grace of God who seems happy to work within our church cultures rather than demanding we do things his way (i.e. Anglican-style!).

Much evaluation of the so-called 'Toronto Blessing' has flowed under the bridge since the halcyon days of the mid-1990s. Some have regarded it as a hysterical outpouring of human emotion that had nothing whatsoever to do with the Holy Spirit, while others have pointed to the fruit in terms of social outreach programmes, intercession, healing and empowering. Some have tried to prove from Scripture that these kinds of manifestations are only to be expected, while others have used the same Scriptures to demonstrate that the whole thing was a satanic plot to corrupt the church. Twenty years on all I can say is that this period of my life was the most fun, the most exciting and the most fulfilling. I can point to changed lives and changed churches, and I cannot but believe that God was doing something especially powerful during those days. Like all 'revivals' there was an inevitable fading, but I have no doubt that the fruit that has remained in my life from this period has lasting value.

I must tell you, or rather complete, one more story from the Coventry days. Not a lot of people know this, but the city is home to one of the finest choirs in the land, the St Michael's Singers. If you've ever watched *Songs of Praise* you'll almost certainly have heard them, either because they will have performed, or because they are interspersed incognito among the 'congregation' (yes, that's why *SoP* always sounds so much better than the singing in your church!). Various people from our church were choir members, including David our organist, and we would occasionally attend performances to support them.

It was a normal Sunday morning: the service had ended and I was waiting in the porch to get told off, when I spotted on our noticeboard a new poster, with details of the next St Michael's Singers concert. Imagine my shock to realise that they were to do Berlioz's *Te Deum*! This was the piece my friend Pam had introduced me to twenty-five years earlier, and which was on my bucket list to hear again. I grabbed David as he came out. 'Get me some tickets for the Berlioz!' I begged, and told him the story of my previous encounter with it at my first prom.

'You know it then?' he asked.

I certainly did: the CD was on my most-played list. He told me that because it is such a vast work they were wanting to draft in some more voices: how would I feel about temporarily joining the St Michael's singers for the performance? 'Lord, now lettest thou thy servant depart in peace!' I exclaimed as I grabbed my diary. David produced the rehearsal schedule, and it was but the work of a few moments to clear my diary, moving a church council meeting and cancelling a couple of weddings. I wasn't just going to hear the *Te Deum*: I was going to sing it!

The *Te Deum* is a Christian hymn of praise dating from the fourth century, and since becoming an Anglican and discovering all things liturgical it has been one of my favourite texts.[14] But Berlioz, himself an agnostic, had a very different purpose for its majestic words: they were both a celebration of the victories of Napoleon, but also, using the contrast between organ and orchestra, a comment on the uneasy relationship between Church and State in nineteenth-century France. I turned up for my first rehearsal with great anticipation.

Not a lot of people know this either, but Coventry Cathedral is like an iceberg, not because the heating system doesn't work, but because there is more of it below ground level than there is above. Underneath the normal bits the public get to see there is a huge labyrinth of rooms and corridors. To make your way to the subterranean cavern where the choir practises you have to go down a spiral staircase, along dark and dusty corridors piled with broken chairs, dead candles, *Books of Common Prayer* and the becobwebbed skeletons of lost choirboys from generations past. The first rehearsal, to which I had so looked forward, was a nightmare. I discovered that there is all the difference in the world between having heard a piece on a CD a few times, and being able to sing it, particularly to the exacting standards required of us. I have sung in choral societies in the past, but had never experienced the sheer exhausting hard work of singing to this standard. Twice a week for the next several weeks we descended into the abyss and note-bashed, went over tricky bits (i.e. most of it) again and again, and gradually, very gradually, saw it coming together. Finally it was time for the 'dress rehearsal' when we would put it all together with the orchestra and the other four choirs involved in this vast project, and sing it *en situ* upstairs in the cathedral itself. When I turned up for the final run-through I was in for a big surprise: we were going to do it backwards.

Because Berlioz had used organ and orchestra to represent the warring powers of the France of his day, they usually play in opposition to each other rather than together. But what I didn't know was that he had written into the directions for the performance of his work that the organ and orchestra were to be sited as far from each other as possible. In one memorable TV performance of the work, from Edinburgh, I believe, this was taken to lengths even Berlioz would not have imagined: the organ was played in a church a mile away from the concert hall and the sound piped through electronically. We couldn't quite manage that, but we did have organ and orchestra at opposite ends of the cathedral. Since orchestras are generally far more mobile than organs, the vergers had turned all 2,000 seats round through 180 degrees, and the audience would face the back of the cathedral. But it was only as I took my seat for the rehearsal to begin that I realised the other implication of this shift. I was going to be singing this astoundingly beautiful music, which had meant so much to me for the last twenty-five years, and these magnificent words of praise to the Trinity, while looking straight into the eyes of the glorified Christ on the huge east wall tapestry. I lost it completely, and was able actually to sing very little through the tears and awe of that occasion, one which I will carry to my grave with me. Fortunately by the evening I had got over it and gave what I felt in my own modest way to be a stunning performance.

We worship God now, and we seek to minister to others in his name, as it were, in the cellars among the muck and dust and broken bits of this life. We get it wrong, we occasionally shout at one another about our bum notes; we often find worship far more hard work than liberating ecstasy; we often feel as though we're completely outclassed and have no right to be there at all. But one day we'll sing our worship songs looking directly into the face of our glorified Lord. I think that apart from the profound emotional buzz of this experience there was something deeper God downloaded into me. As you get older you think more about death, but I think God gave me through the *Te Deum* my first real awareness of heaven as 'home', a destination to be looked forward to rather than feared and avoided. As I sung my praises into the face of my Lord something in me got in touch with a genuine longing for the time when I would do it for real. This life is just rehearsal: bring on the eternal performance!

6

An Unexpected Journey

With hindsight I think a sense of dissatisfaction first became apparent to me in our local, enchantingly called 'The Open Arms', after a meeting of our PCC (Parochial Church Council – the Anglican leadership team in each local church). Everything had gone exceptionally well. I can't now remember what 'everything' was, but it had been a very smooth meeting, and we had agreed whatever it was we had to agree with no trouble and a high degree of unanimity. As I say, I can't remember the details, but what I can remember was one of the churchwardens, as he handed me the pint he'd just bought me, saying 'You've got them eating out of your hands now, haven't you?'

He was right: after the early years in the parish, in which there were the usual battles due to the fact that I was neither perfect nor even as good as my predecessor, I had now won the hearts of most of the people who hadn't left, and they were enjoying and responding to my leadership. Over the last seven years we had seen the advent of charismatic renewal, Wimber-style prayer ministry, a worship band and even a drum kit, the Toronto Blessing and the Alpha course. In other words we were a right-on nineties church, and we were seeing the fruits of growth to prove it. In spite of some people finding it was all too much and leaving for somewhere less exciting, we had about half as many again worshippers as we had had when I arrived. It was all going so well: I should have seen something coming.

As I pondered the warden's comment I realised, much to my surprise, that while I was mightily glad of a slightly quieter life, there was a bit of me that missed the cut and thrust of the early years. I hated to admit it to myself, but maybe life was just a tiny bit boring and lacking in challenge. Everything was running pretty smoothly, and I could not see the need for any more major changes of direction. But I just got on with it: after all I had another six years to go until I moved on.

It is a fairly little-known fact outside the C of E that as part of the Licensing Service for new vicars you have to ring the church bell (if there is one). There is a custom that you give it one dong for every year you think you'll be likely to stay there, and although it is in no way legally binding everyone counts and so gets some idea of the new vicar's intentions. When I went to Coventry I had rung the bell thirteen times, as that would take us up to the time our youngest son left home, although that idea had been scuppered a bit by the arrival of Vicki. She was our unexpected surprise, and was a real delight. I have to admit that I was petrified at the idea of having a daughter. I think we'd done pretty well with two boys, but everyone told me that girls are a different thing altogether. The boys loved her instantly, and she remains a real delight to us. She is far and away the most intelligent member of the family, and is currently applying to medical school to pursue a career as a doctor of some sort. But with her arrival while we were in Coventry we all felt well settled in as a family and ready to keep on keeping on.

A little while later I was talking to our resident saint, an older woman with such a beautiful spirit of prayer and such deep wisdom coming out of a long steady walk with God that had lasted decades. Most churches have one, and Eileen was ours. Everyone loved her, and I would have trusted my life to her and her ability to hear from God. So when she suddenly said to me, 'I don't think you're going to be with us that much longer,' I sat up and took notice. At first I wondered whether she had had some kind of premonition of a nasty accident with a chain-saw or something, but she quickly clarified and said that she had a sense that I would be leaving the parish before too long. I've learnt, of course, that 'words' such as these are to be stored away and pondered, even when given by people like Eileen, so I didn't immediately begin scanning the jobs columns of the *Church Times*, where clergy find their new posts.

Christmas came and went, and on 6 January, which I remember because it was the Feast of the Epiphany, I was away on a conference. We were holding a special act of worship, which included in the liturgy the Methodist Covenant Prayer. This is a prayer of total surrender to God, which in the Methodist church is traditionally used at the start of each New Year as a kind of rededication to the will and purposes of God. It is a lovely but very scary prayer, and I was unprepared for the effect it would have on me.

The prayer begins:

I am no longer my own but yours.
Put me to what you will,

rank me with whom you will;
put me to doing,
put me to suffering;
let me be employed for you,
or laid aside for you,
exalted for you,
or brought low for you . . .[15]

I was joining in like a good congregational member, until I said the line 'exalted for you'. In that moment I heard the voice of God just about as clearly as I have ever heard it. Not audibly, but almost as good as. 'If I wanted to, would you let me exalt you?' God asked me. I was so startled that I jumped off the liturgy and held a conversation with God inside my head while everyone else carried on around me.

'Would you let me exalt you?' he asked again.

Now I had a real problem with this. I know that in the Christian world we are swimming in a very small pond. Over the years I have met a large number of what I call 'Christian social climbers', people who like to be seen hanging out with the latest Christian celebs. It seems to me that there are some people who need to be famous, even if vicariously. Nowadays we see this phenomenon in the multiplicity of 'talent' contests on the telly, and the amount of heat they generate. But the Christian world of the 1990s was no different. I had no desire whatsoever to be a celeb, and most of all I had no desire to be obnoxious. I didn't want to be the kind of person whom people saw coming and got out of the way. So for God to ask me if I was up for a bit of exalting was a very pertinent question. My immediate reaction was to say back 'No way!'

but as I listened to the rest of the congregation around me freely and wholeheartedly yielding all things to God's pleasure and disposal I realised there was a basic incongruity in my response. I can't remember anything about the rest of the service, because God and I were busily discussing his theoretical proposal. I finally arrived at the point where I reluctantly told him that I supposed that if he wanted to he did in fact have the right to exalt me, but that he would have to do it really carefully, as the last thing I wanted was to become an obnoxious Christian celeb. He'd have to work really hard at keeping me humble if he wanted to exalt me.

This was a very powerful experience, particularly coming so much out of the blue, but by the time I got back to the parish I felt as though if I were a plant someone had put a big spade in the ground beside me and given my roots a good loosening. I had come to realise that I was about to go on an unexpected journey, although at this stage I had no idea where or when. This sense of shaking up was reinforced when our church administrator was praying for me a week or so later, and sensed a 'word from the Lord' for me. She knew nothing of my previous conversations with God or Eileen, but she turned me to Joshua 3:7: 'Today I will begin to exalt you in the eyes of [all the people]' and said, 'I've no idea what that means, but I just felt God saying it to you.' I knew all right!

For the next couple of months this happened again and again, as bits of guidance piled on top of each other, all saying the same thing. I've often counselled people that one good way of recognising the voice of God is to look for accumulation, for the same message coming from lots of different directions at the same time. I suppose the classic biblical example of this is the encounter between Peter and Cornelius, which is recorded in Acts 10. God has been communicating with both Cornelius and Peter in very different ways, and when they finally meet up it seems no surprise to anyone. This sense of God working from both ends at once, and his guidance coming from lots of different directions, is far more reliable than one lone 'word' or sense of leading. Well, I got it in spades! Before long I was as certain as anything that we were soon to be on the move. I was curious about how another job would lead to 'exaltation' for me, but that was fine, as I wasn't keen on that bit anyway.

When the letter came, I knew that it was what I had been waiting for. Would I like to consider applying for the job of Director of Anglican Renewal Ministries (ARM), which was soon to become vacant? I responded with a long phone call to one of the trustees, who had been a friend of mine from college, and told her about my root-loosening experiences. She told me in turn that the Director's role was a national travelling ministry of speaking and teaching, furthering ARM's aim of 'promoting appropriate expressions of charismatic renewal in the Church of England' and wider. I would have an office and some back-up staff in Derby, but my job was to travel the country getting the name and vision of ARM out there, supporting those who were struggling to see renewal take root in their churches, and to promote good practice in all aspects of Anglican renewal. In contrast with life in an average parish in the Midlands, this was exaltation indeed.

The application and interview process took its course, and not at all to my surprise I was offered the job, even in spite of my interview presentation on the subject of the hidden theological significance for Anglican renewal of *Teletubbies*, a then newly popular children's television programme in which four humanoid creatures who live with a load of rabbits and a vacuum cleaner in a kind of eco-house in the Cotswolds dance, play and hug each other a lot. In any case Eileen had told me I would be appointed, so that gave me a certain confidence.

The ARM years were a lot of fun, and as well as travelling around England I ventured into Scotland and Wales and, since in terms of Anglican organisation Europe is a part of England (an unusual reversal of current political thinking), into Germany and Switzerland too. There was also a memorable couple of weeks in South Africa with our sister organisation SOMA ('Sharing of Ministries Abroad'). I became a well-known conference speaker and teacher, and I reckon I became a national expert on the relative comforts of various conference centres and retreat houses around the country. I did even consider writing a kind of Egon Ronay Guide to them, and I think I spent more time during those years in other beds than I did in my own at home. I loved driving, and I loved speaking, writing and teaching, so I had five really great years.

My love for driving was useful, since on a couple of occasions I had not handled my diary as effectively as I might have done. One Saturday morning I was to speak in Brighton, but then I was invited to a conference that weekend in Southport. I was to be speaking on Saturday evening, so I had to do a hasty nip up several motorways that afternoon. However, that piece of bad planning pales into insignificance beside another booking disaster in which I finished a training day in Bangor, North Wales at 4 p.m. one Saturday, and I had to preach at 10 a.m. Sunday morning in Truro. Unlike my Brighton to Southport journey, this drive was an unmitigated disaster: leaving the church in Bangor I heard a loud rip and discovered my trousers had split in the worst possible place. Then a few miles down the M6 the exhaust fell off my car, turning me instantly into a noisy boy-racer, and then a speed camera in some roadworks near Bristol flashed me. Fortunately it was one of those cameras with no film in, and the vicar's wife I was visiting in Cornwall did a good repair job on my trousers. After that I learnt to manage my diary more carefully, and even learnt that it was OK to say 'no' to some invitations, enjoyable though they might have been.

But I want to reflect not so much on the work of ARM but on the nature of God's guidance. I don't think I have ever known such a clear sense of God's preparation and call than that experience that got me out of my parish and into ARM. But I also know that I have not known anything like it since and, as you will soon see, I have often been left with a bewildering sense that God isn't at all interested in leading or guiding me.

My call into the parish in Coventry had been very different. I had decided after two four-year curacies that I had had enough of parish ministry, and knew enough about it to be able to be a kind of consultant to others. So I determined I was going to be a Diocesan Mission Advisor or something similar. I set about applying for everything I could find remotely like that kind of a job, and I said to God in a moment of almost total surrender, 'I'll go anywhere you send me apart from Africa or the Midlands.' I got four interviews for diocesan posts, and was beaten each time. By the same person. He kept getting offered the job but turning it down, thus allowing himself to come up against me again the next time. Finally he did take the post, and my options were exhausted. It was just after that that the Bishop of Coventry rang me, and offered me a parish. In the end I gave in and went to have a look at it because I had nothing else in the pipeline, and I was under pressure to move on from my curacy. I gave in and reluctantly took the job, very dejected and cross. It was then that God spoke to me through a fluorescent green toothbrush.

We were about to move out of our house in Sheffield, and I was down at the local parade of shops when I spotted the toothbrush in the window of a hardware shop. It wasn't difficult to spot: it almost glowed. I decided that my boys would love toothbrushes that colour, so I went in and bought a green one and an equally lurid pink one. The delight on their little faces at such an outrageous gift was something to behold. But a few days later, when I spotted one of the toothbrushes in the bathroom, I sensed God speaking to me again. 'This parish in Coventry,' he said, 'is my gift to you. I chose it for you as you chose these toothbrushes for your sons, and I want you to receive it with the delight with which they received your gifts to them.' It was hard to feel that being sent to Coventry was in any way a gift, but I had no doubt that I had heard God speak, and that I had to lose my resentful and disappointed attitude as soon as possible. The next day I went back to the hardware shop, bought myself another green toothbrush, and stuck it in a picture frame (no mean feat). I kept it in my study for the duration of my ministry there, to remind me that, whatever it felt like, this job was actually God's gift to me. There were times when it was a life-saver.

Yet at other times God's voice seemed silent, or at best uninterested. I have taken decisions that seemed to have been based on nothing more than common sense or personal preference. I have longed to hear the voice of God as clearly as I have done in the past. But instead I have felt left entirely to my own devices. So why does God seemingly play these games with us? It is completely natural to believe that the longer we've been seeking to follow Jesus, the easier it will get to hear his voice and obey his guidance, yet the opposite seems to be true. The closer we get to God, and the greater our desire to seek and follow his will for us becomes, the harder it gets actually to hear his voice. I had learnt by now that I was no longer my own, and that my life should be lived according to his plans rather than mine, yet I needed a bit of an upgrade over the whole way that guidance works. I think this is a download that has come in bits over the years, rather than through one dramatic experience. I share my insights in case they might be helpful to you.

I think there are three main things I've learnt about the vexed question of guidance. The first is that sometimes God says to us, 'What do *you* want to do?' I can remember as a young Christian getting fixated on a desperate desire to get everything exactly right, in every smallest detail. I remember a friend at college who apparently used to pray each morning about what colour socks God wanted him to wear that day. Call me cynical, but I could just hear God saying back, 'D'you know? I really don't mind. Why don't you choose?'

This is a silly example, but it betrays a mindset whereby if we don't obey God in every little aspect of our lives, as though there was a set path for us to walk and no room for personal choice, apocalyptic disaster is likely to hit us. Quite rightly Christians are concerned to seek God's will and obey him, but I'm not entirely convinced that he particularly has a will for some of the things over which we agonise. This kind of thinking feels like what I would have engaged in before my breakdown, and frankly I'm glad to have left it behind. As a father I want good things for my kids, and there are some things that if they asked me I would suggest they go for, or avoid. But most of their day-to-day decisions are down to them. I hope I have brought them up to make wise decisions, but if in their thirties they felt the need to ask me about every little thing, I might be forgiven for thinking that there was something wrong. So the first thing I think I would say to anyone agonising over guidance would be to ask themselves 'What do *you* want to do here? What feels right to you? What does common sense suggest?' If you really have the mind of Christ growing in you, surely it ought to be the case that more and more the things Jesus wants chime in with what you want. This is not of course a universal rule, but it ought to apply more as we grow in Christ.

The corollary of this, though, is that we might sometimes get things wrong. But the good news is that under the less neurotic model I'm proposing this isn't the major disaster we might think it to be. When I'm speaking on this I show a slide of one of those children's maze puzzles, you know the kind of thing: Bob the Builder has lost Pilchard his cat, and there is a selection of paths that may or may not lead to him.

You begin to trace one of them, but if it turns out to lead to a dead end you have no option but to go right back to the start and try another one. I make the point that with God it isn't like this. Bob might get close to Pilchard but unable to reach him: so God simply draws another path that opens the way. Even when we get things wrong, in the economy of God, it isn't about going right back to the beginning and starting again: it's about looking for God's redemption. This fact again removes the phenomenal pressure to hear God accurately and follow him exactly every step of the way. If he knows that the sincere intention of our hearts is to follow him obediently, he is perfectly able to let us know if we're going wrong. There's that lovely promise in Isaiah 30:21 that reassures us that God's voice will be heard, whether we turn off to the left or to the right, saying 'This is the way; walk in it', not when things are going well, but when we have already diverted from the path.

So my first counsel would be not to let 'guidance' become a big issue about which to lose sleep. Dedicate your will to God, listen to your heart and allow him to make minor corrections along the way if he needs to.

Secondly, I think I've learnt that God's guidance, when it does come, can come in many more different ways than we might expect. You'll understand that in my Christian background God spoke through Scripture, and that was about it. That is why it was an unwritten law that you had to have a daily 'quiet time' when you read the Bible and prayed. Otherwise how would God be able to communicate with you? There's nothing wrong, of course, with good habits of regular prayer and Bible reading, but actually our lives do not depend on them. The very Bible that we so venerated teaches us that God communicates with his people in a variety of ways, including dreams, visions, trances, a burning bush, angels, other human messengers, audible voices, prophetic words and even a talking donkey. And of course common sense, one of his greatest gifts – at least to some people. So to use the Bible to limit guidance to the Bible is a profound misuse of it. If we expect that God might be speaking to us through our dreams, for example, we will be far more likely to hear him than if we just put it down to that cheese we had for supper.

My third piece of advice, and this is the difficult one, comes from an awareness I've already mentioned, that the longer we have been Christians the less clearly God seems to speak to us. I can only guess why this is, but it is pretty well documented, and certainly rings true in my own experience. Maybe it has something to do with growing up: when our own kids are very young they need us to tell them pretty much everything, but when they're grown up they are capable, hopefully, of leading their own lives. Maybe it's something to do with the mind of Christ growing in us, so that God is able to trust us much more to do the right things instinctively, without the need for angels or burning bushes. Or maybe it's a little bit to do with seeking God: if we're used to him taking the initiative very clearly, as he did in calling me from Coventry to ARM, we can take that a bit for granted, when he would actually like us to spend more time seeking, and even agonising, to hear his voice. I'm not sure about any of this, but I would say that if you have in the past felt God speak clearly to you, but feel that nowadays his guidance is a lot less in evidence, then join the gang: that's how it tends to be. It isn't a sign that God has abandoned you, or that he's lost interest. It's more likely to be that you're growing up and need a lot less of the dramatic guidance you needed when you were a younger Christian.

Having said that, my call to leave ARM was every bit as dramatic as my call into it. It came at 4:10 p.m. on Monday 17 September 2001, a few days after the tragic events of 9/11. I left a trustees' meeting at which we were told that we were in some financial difficulties as an organisation, and walked out to open our annual national conference. There were the old faithful supporters, all looking a year older than they had last year. There were about half the numbers we had hoped for at the conference, and a distinct lack of under fifties. In fact, it looked like church. Somewhere in my head a switch flipped, and I realised that after five years I just didn't want to do this any more. I had started with the aim of helping ARM become an organisation for the next generation of young leaders but, in spite of my best efforts, we had failed to stop the ageing of our clientele, as the younger generation related more naturally to other networks such as New Wine. Meanwhile we were servicing many people who had borne the heat of the battle for renewal in the 1960s and 1970s, but were now mostly retired. That was never the kind of ministry I had wanted, and I had lost heart for it now. That conference was quite difficult for me, as you might imagine, and later on I told the trustees of my decision to move on when my contract was up (in a year's time). Once again I was in the job market.

Meanwhile the trustees began to ask the obvious question 'Who could be our next director?' This led them to think in sequence about the qualities they were looking for, the future strategy of the organisation, the place God might have for it, did God have a place for it, and eventually 'Should we be continuing at all?' After a residential retreat in January 2002 the decision was taken not exactly to close down, but to go into temporary hibernation. ARM ceased to exist, but the baton was handed on a couple of years later to ReSource, (www.resource-arm.net) under the leadership of Martin Cavender. I have noticed over the years that I have an extraordinary gift for closing things down, a much needed skill in a church littered with activities well past their sell-by date, and I have even written a book on how to do it.[16]

7

On the Road Again

It was a hot and dusty day in the city of Derby. I was doing the agencies, but to be honest I wasn't getting very far.

For the past year I had been applying for jobs. I had my first look around just a few weeks after the ill-fated ARM conference, and since then I had been applying for all sorts: parishes, diocesan posts, lecturing, you name it. I got nowhere at all, and time was running out. My contract with ARM had finished at the end of August, although in fact the organisation had closed down at the end of July. I had been told that we could stay in the house as long as we needed to, but my past experiences had taught me that that might prove to be an empty promise, which in fact it did.

So faced with unemployment, the end of my stipend and possible homelessness, I decided that I had to find gainful employment in a context outside the church.

'Is there anything else you can do?' asked the man in yet another temping office. He looked slightly bemused, poor chap. After all, it can't be every day you get faced with an out-of-work vicar looking for a job. He didn't have anything on his books that was *directly* linked with being a vicar, but give him his due: he really was trying. I think he felt just a little bit sorry for me.

'What have you done in the past?' he persisted. At least he *was* persisting: most of the others had just laughed. Dredging mentally through my CV, I tried my job in pharmacy in the early 1970s, a job that bore the flattering title of 'Sterile Technician'. I had worked for a year at a hospital in the East End of London, followed by another year in industry, making up sterile fluids for drips and injections. But it was no good. Apparently sterile technicians were in about as much demand as vicars in the city of Derby.

'I've done loads of clerical work,' I tried hopefully. As a student I had worked for a well-known mail-order catalogue, in the 'indecipherable addresses' department. It was my job to guess whether the scrawl on the order form actually said NP20 or GU3, or whether 'Mrs Jones, Swansea' really lived anywhere with any detail meaningful enough actually to allow us to deliver anything to her, because the handwriting wasn't all that clear.

But the highlight of my clerical (office, not clergy) career had been ten weeks as a student with a well-known car manufacturer. I was at the 'Research and Development' plant, so I had been sure it would all be very exciting. The plant was huge and luxuriously equipped, and there were all sorts of fascinating things to wander round and see during breaks. Lots of machines opened and shut car doors or boots twenty-four hours per day, or pressed up and down on seat springs, to study the long-term effects of wear and tear. There was even one of those tracks where they deliberately crashed vehicles into brick walls to monitor the effects on the unfortunate dummies who were inside. My job, however, was slightly less interesting. I had to take delivery of large piles of paper, printed on one side with details about the planned design changes to the latest models. I had to write the date on each bit of paper, and then throw it in the bin. At the end of the day a man would come round and empty the bins, carting the contents off to be burnt. Now you know why your car is so expensive.

So what about office work? Might there be a job for me there? I know clergy are not always totally in touch with the real world, but I felt pretty certain that with time and appropriate training I would be able once again to hold down some kind of responsible and worthwhile job involving dating and binning. I was also highly computer-literate nowadays: perhaps I could get a job in the cyber-equivalent of my car industry role, typing stuff and then deleting it? And every evening just before I went home I could empty my recycle bin. Someone must want me for that kind of work. Sadly, they didn't.

'Then I used to drive,' I remembered. Agency-man's eyes lit up.

'Drive?'

'Delivering surgical instruments to hospitals.' I had had a job, again in the 1970s, with a pharmaceutical company that had a surgical offshoot. For three years I had roamed the hospitals of the land, including most of those in central London, carrying in the back of my van all those kinds of things surgeons shout out for in *Holby City* and *Casualty*. In fact I did enter the glamorous world of TV for real: my firm won the contract with the BBC for an earlier hospital series called *Angels*, which some of my more wrinkly readers might remember. I had to deliver van-loads of props for the series to the BBC Television Centre in Wood Lane, but sadly I never met anyone any more famous than the storekeeper.

After a while I moved to an offshoot of the same company, which specialised in syringes and sutures. The highlight of this part of my career was undoubtedly the mercy-dash from London to a hospital in the East Midlands where a patient was open on the operating table before anyone realised they had completely run out of the stuff for sewing him up again. The Managing Director of the company, who drove a top-of-the-range white Capri, told me to take his car and get the stuff there as fast as I could. The firm would pay my speeding fines. So I stuck a notice in the back window that said 'Urgent – Medical supplies', turned the headlights on full beam, and went for it. So convincing was my performance that a police car pulled out of my way and let me shoot past him somewhere on the North Circular. I think the patient lived, and I didn't get a fine, which in a way was really annoying, because since then I've had one for doing a lot less than the speeds I got up to that day, and I didn't have the firm to pay it for me, the Church of England being quite reticent in such matters.

Commercial driving experience? Agency-man's heart became strangely warmed. At last we were motoring. I could get a job driving! Before long I had undergone a training session in the use of tachographs (not invented when I worked as a driver before), and had been equipped with Totector safety boots, a fluorescent yellow waistcoat and an introductory card for my new employer. I had got a job! My joy was unrestrained. My family were not going to starve after all. We would not have to send Vicki out sweeping chimneys;

Chris wouldn't have to take in washing. I was to be a proper breadwinner again. No more living by faith: I had employment!

As soon as I got home to announce the good news to the family, though, I began to have doubts. I was to restart my career as a driver after a pause of twenty-six years, but would I be up to it? Even when I had driven professionally before, it was in Bedford vans the size of Transits – 18 cwt, I think they were in those days. Sometimes if there was a particularly large load we took out the Luton Transit, but at a mere 35 cwt that was still pretty small. And anyway, who knows what a hundredweight is nowadays?

But now I was to drive 7.5 tonne trucks. Just how big was 7.5 tonnes in English money? How much, indeed, was one tonne? Was it the same as a good honest English ton only spelt in the European way? I couldn't really picture it, but seven and a half of them sounded big to me. Apparently they'd changed the law sometime in the mid-1990s so that anyone could drive up to 7.5 tonnes on a normal car licence as long as they had passed their test before a certain date, which I had by about 20 years. Surely if you could drive it on a car licence it wouldn't be *that* big.

Then out of the blue I got a phone call from a friend at church. I'd been a van driver in the past, hadn't I? Was I free Friday? (Well, I certainly wouldn't be doing any vicaring.) They were putting a new lighting rig in the church and it needed picking up from High Wycombe, but some of the poles were four metres long so they would have to hire a special long wheelbase van, which they could only get on Friday when every normal person would be at work. Would

I be able to run the van down and do the pick-up? Of course I agreed, secretly glad of the opportunity to do some van driving before the big day on Monday.

I duly turned up Friday morning, to find my vehicle, which looked to a Transit van like a stretch limo looks to a Mondeo. Gingerly I climbed in and started the engine, but before I'd reached the end of the road I knew it was going to be OK. It was like swimming: once you've learnt it, you can never forget it. I even stopped for a bag of chips on the way, to prove I could still do that. By the time I got to High Wycombe I was a proper van driver again, and I loved it. Roll on Monday. Goodbye hundredweights: bring on the 7.5 tonners: I could do this!

It was still with some trepidation that the following Monday I was rudely awakened by my alarm at 5 a.m. Nevertheless, as I drove the twenty-five minute journey to the depot I prayed, as you do, not just that God would look after me, but also for opportunities to be a good witness, and to show the love of Christ to those among whom I was to work.

I turned into the depot at 5:50 a.m., and stopped at the gatehouse. The firm was a well-known national logistics company, and at this particular depot they handled deliveries for several large stores such as Marks and Spencer, and – my division – IKEA. I signed in, had my car registration number noted, was given my pass onto the site, and was directed down to the bottom of the yard. I had been told whom to ask for: I would find him in the office on the side of the warehouse.

The depot had been an old army barracks, and several large hangar-sized warehouses were dotted about the place. Each had half a dozen or so loading bays, complete with a little set of traffic lights to tell you when it was safe to drive off without taking a forklift and its driver out for the day with you, handy as I was to discover this might have been. As I parked the car I noticed a collection of about thirty huge white trucks parked just round the corner. They must be the ones for the real drivers, I decided, people with HGV licences. I wondered where they parked the 7.5 tonners. I couldn't seem to see any.

I walked into the IKEA office. Imagine the scene. Twenty or thirty men ranging in age from eighteen to over sixty and arrayed, as I was, in fluorescent vests, stood around waiting for their orders for the day. Some were laughing raucously in groups; some were perusing page three of The Sun (or worse), all were swearing fluently and profusely. Most of them were built as though they could carry a bed-settee under each arm up eight flights of stairs without breaking a sweat, forty roll-ups and two greasy breakfasts a day notwithstanding. My prayer for witness quickly turned into a prayer for survival.

Initially and mercifully no-one took much notice of me. It was no big deal; temps came and went almost daily, I discovered, and were not a great cause of excitement among the regulars. But it wasn't very long at all before I did gain some curiosity value. The manager was working systematically down his list, and before long the inevitable happened: he got to me. When he shouted across the room for 'The Reverend Leach!' I realised that Agency-man had told them all about me. My reputation had gone before. In that moment I was instantly and dramatically outed. There was a vicar on the crew! I was an immediate celebrity. A strange silence filled the office, as all eyes turned in my direction. If there had been someone playing a honky-tonk piano in the corner, they would have stopped instantly. The silence was broken by a small outbreak of Gregorian chant from some wags in one corner. I smiled nervously around the room, trying to look as if I did this every day.

Initially there were a couple of misunderstandings to clear up. 'Are you really a Reverend?' I was asked, both then and constantly for the duration of my stay there. I told them I was, but they still thought I was having a laugh. 'Why on earth would anyone want to pretend they were a vicar, if they weren't really and they weren't going to a fancy dress party?' I asked. They could see my point.

The other misunderstanding was more serious. One of the bosses had also come from a professional background, but had been struck off for a serious misdemeanour, and so was now working in the transport office. This was common knowledge among the staff, so of course my arrival posed a whole new question. Why should a vicar turn up for work here? There could only be one reason: he'd been at the choir-boys. Either that or he'd been helping himself from the collection plate. Which was it? I reassured them that it was neither. I was just between jobs, resting.

In fact I didn't get very much at all in the way of rest. I was in at the deep end. The boss, who looked not unlike Groucho Marx, took pity on me, and told me that for the first couple of weeks I could go out with the other drivers as a porter/navigator, so I'd get to know the ropes a little bit before I'd actually do any driving. That suited me fine, as I had discovered that the trucks I had seen on the way in were indeed ours. They were the 7.5 tonners, and they looked absolutely massive to me. I'd certainly never driven anything remotely that big before, apart from one short, illegal and uninsured journey many years ago, the details of which need not hold us up now.

I was about to become a professional driver once again.

I was introduced to Pete, my partner for my first day. He would, I was told, take good care of me, and he did. While we waited for the truck to be loaded, he showed me how to map out our route, which was around Leicestershire, and mercifully not too long a journey. We were given a computer printout with the approximate route on it, typically about 12 to 15 drops weighing all in all about 2.5 tonnes. The sheet contained all the addresses in approximate order, a contact phone number, and details, including the weight of the stuff to be delivered. I had to locate the houses on the A-to-Z, and work out how we'd get from one to the next, and whether in fact the computer had put them in the best order. Computers tended not to know about the latest roadworks, or the traffic jam blackspots to avoid, or the bridges under which a 7.5 tonner would not fit. Most of the drops were at private houses, although a few were to shops, factories or offices, and one or two went to the docks for export. I was to discover that they were the best ones: a forklift simply came and took the pallet load off in one go while we sat and watched. Sadly they were few and far between, and most of the time everything had to be unloaded by hand and, on a bad drop, carried upstairs. I was going to have lots of opportunities to find out what a tonne felt like.

Eventually Pete and I set off, and all in all we had a good day. We got on well, I found I could lift most things, and I navigated well and efficiently, apart from one small section where I took him by mistake down a country lane just about wide enough to get the truck through. Pete seemed genuinely interested in me, and in why a vicar should be working delivering IKEA furniture. Conversation was easy, and once we were on the motorway home he allowed me to have a kip, my navigating done. I felt I'd earned it. I was impressed with how much allowance he made for me, knowing it was my first day on the job: I had expected a kind of sink-or-swim approach from the experienced hands.

Eventually we rolled back into the yard, but we hadn't finished yet. We had to fill the truck up with diesel from the depot's own private pump, and we had to back up to a huge skip to empty out all the cardboard, polystyrene, clingfilm and plastic bags that had been the packing for the goods we had delivered. Then we had to go back to the office to hand in our tachos, fill in umpteen forms and return our phones, petrol agency cards and borrowed maps. Only then were we free to clock off, although as we were paid by the quarter of an hour it was often worth hanging around with another coffee to make it up to the next fifteen minutes. Coffee cost 17p, but it would mean another £1.50 on our wages, so it seemed a good investment. Then there was the twenty-five minute drive home. I got in that evening exhausted but happy. All in all I needn't have worried; this was going to be OK. I hadn't really done much in the way of evangelism, or driving for that matter, but it was early days, I told myself as I drifted off to sleep. I was pacing myself.

8

A Day in the Life

The next morning the 5 a.m. alarm was slightly less of a shock, although still a rude awakening. I drove to the depot feeling a lot more confident. I knew where to go, I had learnt at least a few of the ropes, and I was looking forward to another day of navigating, healthy exercise and good conversation. I was in for a shock.

As I reported for duty to the boss, he pointed across the room to Carl. 'He's your porter for today,' I was told. Surely some mistake? I'm the porter, he must be the driver. No, he's only 18 and he's a temp, a student. You're in the driving seat today. Thus it was on my second morning that I found myself climbing into the cab of an Iveco 7.5 tonne truck to continue my deliverance ministry in the wilds of the Tamworth area. In fact, as with my stretch tranny the previous Friday, I soon found that it wasn't too bad. Once you understand the principles, you can drive pretty much anything with a rigid chassis (articulated lorries are, of course, a different matter, but my life has never brought me into the driving seat of one of them). The problem that day wasn't the truck or its driver, but its navigator, the dopey student who simply hadn't a clue. He was of course in great awe of me, the professional driver (I 'forgot' to mention to him that it was my first day driving) and was eager to please, but he had obviously never seen a map in his life before, let alone read one. The classic line, as we shot past the turn-off for the third time, was 'I thought you knew where you were going!' I have to confess that I lost my temper with him just a teeny bit, and I felt rotten about it for days afterwards.

We got home late that evening.

But by the third day I felt that I had relaxed into the routine. I was again at the wheel, but fortunately not with Carl, who disappeared without trace, possibly because of what I said when the boss asked me the previous evening how he'd got on, or possibly because of the horrid way the nasty driver had spoken to him.

A typical day had its pattern and looked like this: we'd clock on at 6 a.m. and wait around the depot for our trucks to be loaded. The time would be spent mapping the route from copious numbers of A-to-Zs, drinking what called itself 'coffee' from the machine in the corner, nipping out into the yard for a smoke, another look at page three, a few obscene jokes and another fag (I only did the mapping and the coffee bits, in case you were wondering). Then finally we were loaded and ready to go. It might be a two-hour drive to Manchester, or even further to Aberystwyth or Newcastle-on-Tyne. Then there would be a dozen or more drops, during which the driver and porter between them would shift up to two and a half tonnes of furniture, soon-to-be-fitted kitchens and household appliances. Finally we'd drive home again, to be told who we'd be out with the next day, and where we'd be going. On a good day we might be back at home by 7:30 p.m., but occasionally it could be as late as 10:30. And so to bed, ready for the 5 a.m. alarm the next morning.

So how was a fat and flabby charismatic vicar managing to adapt to his new lifestyle? A few days in, the transport manager told me not to worry about the lads. There might be a lot of bravado and a bit of swearing (a *bit*? Every other word!) but I'd find as many true Christians here as anywhere else. I'd done lots of funeral and baptism visits, so I was well used to the term 'Christian' being watered down to mean 'quite nice', so I nodded sagely and thanked him for his concern. Of course there was quite a lot of the expected ribbing, but it did genuinely seem to be good-natured. They would burst into Gregorian chant when I walked into the room, for example, or talk to me in mock Authorised Version Old Testament. But it was when we were out on the road that some of the 'good Christian' behaviour began to come to the fore. I had obviously been concerned about my physical ability to pull (or rather lift) my weight on the job. I was sure they'd regard me as a bit of a weed (not completely unfairly) and I didn't want them to feel they were carrying me. But I was unprepared for the genuine care they showed to me. 'Your muscles will develop in a few weeks,' one guy told me, 'but in the meantime don't overdo it. Leave the really big stuff for me.' Or, 'You won't be able to manage that on your own – wait and let's do it together.'

As 'the really big stuff' went, the mother and father of them all was the 4 metre worktop. Weighing in at anything up to 96 kg, these monsters were designed to be cut up and fitted in kitchens. Sadly they weren't cut up before we delivered them, which meant that we had to carry them in whole. The only consolation was that usually (although not always) people had their kitchens on the ground floor. Even with two of us these beasts were a struggle: they were just too wide to tuck under your arm and carry as you might, for example, a ladder, so they had to be carried in front of you, which meant one of you walking backwards. I watched in amazement one day as my mate, an experienced IKEA deliverer, shouldered all 4 metres himself and took it inside single-handed. I immediately took this up as my challenge: one day I would carry a 4 metre worktop on my own.

The other items that filled us with dread were fitted bedrooms and sofa beds. Wardrobes came flat-packed, but almost always had to go upstairs and were really big and awkward. And sofa beds were full of steel working parts with nowhere really to grip them. I never met anyone who could lift one of them on his own.

The company was good, and it wasn't long before I began to believe they were actually a great bunch of blokes. I was trying, too, to be a great bloke, but it was towards the end of my first week in the job when I was sent out with Brian that it began to have real impact. Brian was in his mid-twenties, not the fastest truck in the fleet, not least, it was suggested to me, because of the way he had messed his head up smoking so much dope. He had few friends, was depressive and the night before had told the manager that he wanted to leave at the end of the week because he hated working there so much. No-one liked being partnered with him, so it was only fair that I should get my turn. Perhaps the boss decided a day with the vicar would kill or cure him.

All day I treated him with the care I hope I would show to anyone. Of course I didn't mind him smoking in the cab, but no thanks, I didn't. I bought him a cup of tea at the caff on the A38, we had a bit of a laugh, we appreciated together the beauty of one or two young ladies we passed and, by the end of the day, I found I quite liked him. We went to his native Birmingham, and I found him an excellent and proactive navigator, and a strong and hard worker. He was tall, thin and wiry, with wispy stubble on his face and a perpetual baseball cap glued onto his head. He didn't look that much, but I discovered that he could really lift furniture. It was a good day, and he was a vast improvement on my dopey student. We said goodnight warmly as we clocked off and went our separate ways.

'What on earth did you do to Brian yesterday?' demanded the manager the next morning as I checked in for the day. Although he was a hardened and somewhat cynical man, who had driven more miles himself in the past that he cared to remember, I had noticed that he had a soft spot for the younger lads, most of whom he pastored with a fatherly concern. If I had done anything to upset Brian, I would have him to answer to. I racked my brains, but couldn't think of any way I could have hurt him. I assured the boss I hadn't done anything at all that I knew about. Why? What was the problem?

'He's come back a completely different person!' said the boss. 'He was thinking of leaving yesterday, but now he wants to stay. I've never seen him so happy. I don't know what you said to him, but it's done the trick. Well done!'

On reflection I think I had done something to him. I had treated him well, that is to say I hadn't sworn at him every few minutes throughout the day, which is far more like what he was used to. I hadn't particularly gone out of my way to be nice to him, or to handle him with kid gloves: I'd just treated him as I hope I'd treat anyone (dopey students excepted, of course). My Christian faith was apparently beginning to make a difference to the place; I seemed to have been accepted in spite of it, and apart from good-natured ribbing (that I was able to give as well as receive) I seemed not to have made any enemies. People were still wary of me, of course, and I was still something of a curiosity, but the more people I spent days with, the more word got around that I was OK really. In a moment of spiritual weakness I began to wonder whether God might just have put me there for a purpose.

A few days later I went out with Gary. He was new, from a different agency, and since I had now been there for a week or more I had become part of the furniture. New people were always warned about me, of course: 'Watch it – you're with the vicar today! He'll try to convert you, so don't weaken and give in. And make sure you've got some loose change for when he passes the collection plate round the cab!'

Gary's first question to me as we got into the truck was immediate and aggressive: 'Are you the kind of vicar who doesn't believe anything?' I'm not sure whether the fact that I was working delivering IKEA stuff might have given him the sense that I'd lost my faith or something, or whether he still remembered a past Bishop of Durham. But I was able, at his insistence, to reassure him that I did still believe in things, and in answer to his questioning I was able to tell him some of the things I believed in, and why. What began as a somewhat suspicious and hostile question turned into a genuine enquiry about what made me tick as a Christian. The evangelism that I had been dreading had begun, and it had seemed as natural as talking about my family or Gary's pet cats.

Then there was Greg. He was dapper, about 40, always wore a tie and smart zippy jacket, and carried his complete national set of pristine A-to-Zs, along with the sandwiches that his wife lovingly made him each day, in a neat little aluminium flight case. One unwritten law of the depot was never to ask Greg if you could borrow one of his maps. There was usually a pretty good trade in A-to-Zs as any given crew would need at most two different ones in a day, and were happy to lend out others, but not so with Greg. His were jealously guarded and for his use only. His trousers were always pressed, his glasses polished and his hair neatly trimmed. He was polite to customers (although like the others he could make some choice comments about some of them after we left) and his one passion in life was Saab cars. He drove one of them, an A1-condition saloon that was obviously his pride and joy, but he had many others, he confided to me, on little shelves in his hall at home, courtesy of Messrs Corgi and Dinky. He was quite the best navigator on the crew and, like many of the lads, remarkably strong for his size and unassuming appearance. And he didn't smoke, an added bonus when you have to spend all day in a cab together. I don't really remember what we talked about on our first day out, but I'll never forget what he said as we drove back into the yard.

'I've got a confession to make,' he started, as we headed for the rubbish skip. 'I was (blank) gutted when I found out last night that I was going out with you today. Stuck in a cab all day with a (blank) vicar: I wouldn't be allowed to swear at all. But it's been OK – we've had a (blank) great time, haven't we?' Gratified that I had not in any way curbed his enjoyment of some good invective, I realised that I was obviously smashing a few caricatures. For a Christian to be considered OK seemed like a rare accolade indeed, and I felt gently proud of myself.

Then there were the girls in the office. As we went out each day every truck was equipped with a mobile phone. If anything untoward happened at a particular drop, we had to phone in and report it. Perhaps there was a bit missing, or one of the cupboard doors was the wrong colour or the wrong size. Perhaps they'd ordered a washing machine but we turned up with a doorknob – you know the sort of thing. You've probably experienced it yourself, although of course not from IKEA, it goes without saying.

So there were three girls who sat all day at the other end of the phones to receive our calls (from just about every single drop, as it happened). I can remember the day I made an impact there too.

'Good morning, this is John Leach on route B56,' I explained cheerfully down the phone. 'Drop no. 2, name of Harvey: there's a bed frame missing. Could you look into it for me when you get a moment, please?' I was about to read out the reference number of the offending piece, when I was interrupted.

'You're the vicar, aren't you?' said the girl on the phone. Oh dear. Was my parsonical voice so pronounced that it even gave me away down the phone? Had I been taking Evensong for so long that it had permanently scarred my vocal cords?

'Yes, I am,' I replied. 'How could you tell?'

'Because you're not like the others: you're always nice to us when you phone in.' Indeed I was, in that unlike most of the others I didn't swear at them, blame them personally for not having loaded the bed with their own bare hands, nor make obscene suggestions about what I'd like to do to them after work on the aforementioned bed. They of course were perfectly capable of giving as good as they got over the phones but, even to them, whom I had not even met face to face, something about me communicated positively, and therefore communicated positively, I hoped, about vicars, the church and, ultimately, God.

I did get to meet the girls eventually, and all in all I felt a bit sorry for them, stuck in a man's world. Like all of us they had to wear safety boots and fluorescent jackets at all times, which, to be perfectly honest, didn't show them off at their best. And to have as your sole job dealing with problems, cheeky drivers and irate customers can't have been easy. I made it a rule that I would be as nice to them as I possibly could whenever we came into contact. They seemed to appreciate it.

By now I was very definitely on the team, an accepted member of the crew. As I went out with people each day they became both more relaxed with me and more intrigued by me. They wanted to tell me about their brushes with church, good and bad, and they wanted to know what I thought about gay priests, evolution, divorce, Methodists and other such controversial subjects. They told me of attacks from either evangelicals or Jehovah's Witnesses (not much difference between the two in their book) who doorstepped them, thumped Bibles and told them off. They told me about the joys and sorrows of their families, and showed me photos of their kids. Virtually every day I was there we had some kind of a spiritual and/or pastoral conversation, and in every case they, not me, initiated it. What began as cowardice soon became a firm principle: I would never begin a conversation about God. Yet most days we had one anyway. Much to my surprise, people wanted to talk about God. They were genuinely interested in my life, my career, what I liked and hated about life as a vicar. And they were particularly interested in funerals.

We're all different, aren't we? I think there was an old Pete and Dud sketch about what's the worst job in the world. To me the answer to that is crystal clear: being a gynaecologist or midwife. I know some people have to do it, but for me anything to do with babies is my equivalent of Room 101. Even sitting here typing the word sends shudders down my spine. Second to that would be driving a large truck through tiny streets in Manchester and having to leap out of the cab every now and then to try to stick wing mirrors back on parked cars. But in first place, definitely gynaecology.

But I discovered that I am somewhat unusual in this respect. For many people, including a significant sample of IKEA delivery drivers, the worst job in the world would be taking funerals. I can even remember subscribing to this view myself while I was at college. I knew it was part of the package, but I naively believed that if I was careful I might be able to avoid it in my future ministry. This aversion was not helped by the first funeral I ever attended, which was not that of a relative or friend, but was during my placement when I was attached to a parish priest in Sunderland for some shadowing and work experience. The first funeral that came in while I was there was of a 6-month old baby who had died of a cot death. The young couple had been trying for six or seven years for a baby, and with great joy it was announced that the woman had finally conceived. All went very smoothly, and their son was thriving, until one day he started a baby-sized snuffly cold. Within days he was tragically snatched from them. I didn't hear a lot of the service, because the vicar's voice didn't carry very well above the loud and constant howling of the parents. Thankfully I've only had to do one baby funeral in over twenty years of ministry but that one was a baptism of fire.

I have done something approaching a thousand funerals in all, and it is just about my favourite part of being a priest. It is a real privilege to be a part of people's loss and grief, and to feel that the way I treat them, and the things I say (or don't say) can make a real and lasting difference to them.

I lost count of the number of times my trucking mates asked me about this. They didn't really know much about what vicars actually did all day, of course, and I had my fair share of the usual 'you-only-work-one-day-a-week' jokes. But they did know we took funerals, and they were fascinated to hear about it from my point of view. They couldn't possibly understand how anyone might actually *enjoy* such a harrowing ministry, which I can understand perfectly because I have the same problem with gynaecologists. But as I began to explain the real rewards of bereavement ministry, and that it was OK being with people who were crying once you knew the best way to treat them, they began to see my point, and their admiration for me went up by leaps and bounds. I wasn't just one of the lads, although by now I was, well and truly. I was a lot deeper than meets the eye. I was beginning to intrigue them.

9

Making a Difference

Being by now an old hand at IKEA, I had become
friends with most of the guys and I had even had some
positive contact with the constant stream of temps
who came and went. But there was one person who still
struck fear into my heart. Tom Hollick was over 60, grizzled
and cynical, the most foul-mouthed person in the room (and
that took some doing), humourless and always moaning
about life, the universe and everything. He seemed to regard
work and the management with all the bitterness of someone
trapped in a dead-end job for far too long. He was the only
one of the lads who consistently refused to wear safety boots,
and turned up come rain or shine in a pair of grubby white
trainers. They would have been no use at all if he had dropped
a flat-pack on his toes: on several occasions I was grateful for
my steel Totectors. He looked not unlike Van Gogh's picture
of his friend Dr Gachet but with a much bigger moustache.
In fact his moustache was even bigger than mine, which
really does take some doing, and considerably more tatty and
tobacco-stained. I so hated him! He did the trunking run to
Newcastle a couple of days a week, which didn't involve any
lifting, as it was all handled on pallets by forklifts. That meant
that he usually went out on his own, which suited me just

fine. That was until the inevitable evening when I returned to the depot to find my name with his on the board for the next day. This was not going to be fun. I didn't sleep well that night.

'You're the vicar, aren't you?' he asked as we were driving through the yard to the gatehouse. I braced myself and admitted that indeed I was. 'I've been wanting to talk to you.'

Now what was I in for? If he hated the church and all it stood for anywhere near as much as he appeared to hate everyone and everything else, I was going to spend the day getting a really severe ear-bashing. However, I was in for even more of a shock than I had worried about in my worst nightmares.

'I did that Alpha course last year,' Tom admitted with as much of a coy grin as he could manage. It looked as if it were costing him a considerable amount of effort. In spite of the grin, I felt I was in for an in-depth critique of the whole process. Perhaps I was the first person he had been able to share his insights with, and I was going to get the full spiteful vitriol of his totally negative experience. Oh well, in for a penny . . .

'What did you think of it?' I asked, on the basis that if he was going to hit me it would be better before we got onto the motorway.

'It was absolutely [expletive deleted] brilliant!' I wasn't quite expecting that, and I pondered just for a moment exactly what Nicky Gumbel would have made of this accolade.

'Tell me more,' I prompted, and for the next twenty minutes I got a blow-by-blow account, liberally peppered with words designed to illustrate clearly just how much he had enjoyed the whole experience. I listened open-mouthed as he told me how much he'd enjoyed both the material and the discussion, what a friendly crowd they were, what a turn-around it had brought in his life, and how he and his wife now went to church each Sunday. But even that wasn't the end of his excitement.

'We've got this woman who does that "singing in tongues" in the church,' he confided. 'It's bloody beautiful!' I was able to be enthusiastic and share in his wonder at this wonderful gift, and to admit that I could do that too, although nobody had as yet described my singing as beautiful – an admission that filled him with even more awe for this strange vicar who had suddenly dropped into his life. I wondered how many other clergy with whom he might by chance have found himself stuck in a cab for ten hours could so easily have deflated him with scorn at the 'so-called' working of the Holy Spirit or by putting him right with a theological treatise proving that spiritual gifts were not for today. Tom showed me the Bible he brought to work each day to read in his tacho-breaks, and told me how he didn't always find it easy to understand and what did I think about such-and-such a passage? It would have been such a help to have someone else at work he could ask. Finally, with great wistfulness, he said, 'I really wish I didn't swear so much, but I just can't help it.'

During the day he told me, almost with tears in his eyes, about a heart-breaking situation in his family and a huge decision he had to make. 'Will you pray for me about it?' he asked.

Our route that day was around the Derby area, where I lived, and we popped home for a cup of tea mid-morning.

Tom managed not to swear at my wife; in fact he was friendly and polite, a side of him that certainly didn't come out at work. We carried on our way refreshed, and I marvelled that the first and only colleague I had invited home was the one of whom I had been most terrified.

Tom and I never again found ourselves paired up, but we kept in touch in the depot and I was able to ask him sensitively how things were going as we bumped into one another from time to time. I still remember to pray for him now and again, for his witness in a very difficult environment, and for the growth of his sanctification!

I could write a whole book about my trucking days, but I need to return to the point. Although I tell the story light-heartedly, and there was some genuine fun, I was actually undergoing a real spiritual crisis at the time. The problem of unemployment had been solved by my temporary job, but the spectre of homelessness was looming, as the day drew nearer when we had to move out of the house that had gone with our previous post. But more serious still was the spiritual crisis that had been gestating slowly inside me, and that had now almost come to term. It felt as though God had thrown us on the scrap heap, and the more we prayed the more silent he seemed. This feeling of total powerlessness and abandonment was something I had never experienced before, and in fact it was to be nearly two more years before I was finally offered a new permanent post, two years that I had to live through with a continual sense of abandonment.

Meanwhile, though, I was definitely learning and growing. I think there were two important downloads that came out of this period of my life, one negative and one positive. They are things that have stayed with me and shaped my subsequent ministry, and I remain so grateful to God that, while he wasn't actually answering any of my prayers for a job, a home and some security, he was nonetheless clearly at work through me, downloading into me another important upgrade.

The negative lesson showed me the complete irrelevance of much of church life, in the culture of which I was now steeped, to normal working blokes. As I prayed for and sought sensitively to witness to the guys with whom I was working, I couldn't help but try to picture them in the church that I attended. It was a real shock to me to realise what an immense cultural barrier they would have to cross, and an even bigger one that it should have been a shock to me. I had become so immersed in the system that I had failed to see its bankruptcy.

These were not the hardened bunch of ruffians and petty criminals I had expected before I started at IKEA: they were normal blokes with girlfriends, wives and families, with hobbies and lives outside the cab. And yet the church to which I had devoted so many years of my life seemed to be completely irrelevant to them. I began to appreciate the 'Fresh Expressions' movement in the church that had evolved out of just such a conviction: apparently even if all the churches of the land were thriving and growing we would only ever manage to reach 25 per cent of the population. 'Fresh Expressions' of church were designed to do exactly what it says on the tin: to research and provide some new models that would reach people groups currently untouched by more traditional churches. Deliberately targeting young families, skaters,

Goths, bikers, elderly people, etc. these experimental congregations are well documented and well researched. I began to wonder what Truck Driver Church might look like.

It was never going to be easy to organise such a thing. The only time we had in common was the 6 a.m. start. Nothing could happen any later, as there was no telling when anyone would arrive back at the depot, and the first thing they would want to do then was go home. So I reckoned that the only way interested people could meet would be at 5:30 for half an hour before clocking on. Fortunately I wasn't there long enough to get anything this radical off the ground, but I reckon that with time we could have seen a small group getting together at the start of the day. I was certainly attracting enough interest.

The second lesson for me was about the nature of evangelism. Just what does it mean to 'evangelise'? The lads at the depot seemed to know all too clearly, and they enjoyed telling me of those brushes they had had in the past with either Jehovah's Witnesses or keen evangelical Christians whom they felt were 'out to get them'. The guys' stories were pretty painful to hear, but like many home truths I was the better for having heard them.

But what really struck me was the fact that I had never heard such truths before, and neither, I suspected, had most of the church. Of all the organisations I have ever known, the church is undoubtedly the best at playing 'Let's Pretend'. Partly it comes from our laudable desire to have faith and look on the bright side, a policy with the pleasant side effect of saving us the pain of admitting to failure. But nowhere is this game played hardest than in the area of evangelism. It might be summarised by the old joke about the fisherman returning from a day's sitting by the lake. 'Did you catch any fish?' he is asked. 'No,' he replies, 'but I had good conversations with a few.'

But far worse than this kind of institutionalised dishonesty is the complete inability of the church to own up to the fact that at least some of its evangelism has worked in totally the wrong way. I was hearing so painfully in the cab each day about a kind of evangelism that is culturally insensitive, unhelpfully intrusive and above all is not based on the kind of relationships that are vital in a post-modern world. There are stories, of course, of people who have come to faith through street preachers (manic or ordinary), door-knockers or pub-invaders, and of course in his mercy God is able to use even the well-meaning but misguided attempts of Christians for his ends. But we have sadly made the exceptions into the rules and sought to prove that such antisocial behaviour is actually good evangelism. What a tragic indictment of the church (or at least some bits of it): we have succeeded, by our attempts to draw people towards God, in driving them even further away.

There is some good news and some bad news about this. The good news is that the vast majority of Christians would sooner put their heads in vices and squeeze them slowly than engage in street preaching or other unhelpful 'evangelistic' behaviour. The bad news, though, is that they are often left feeling guilty because of this. If you have never knocked on a door in your life, don't feel left outside: you have probably helped countless people to enjoy their telly without fear of Bible-thumping interruption. If you've never preached in the market-place, thank God. No-one would've listened anyway, so think how much time you've saved yourself, time much better spent in befriending a neighbour or work colleague.

I blame what I was taught in the past about evangelism. Like many evangelicals I had been brought up to feel guilty about the whole business. We knew we had to do it, but we were warned solemnly from the pulpit, time and time again, about how difficult it was going to be. I remember my daughter's first trip to the dentist. We had tried to make it sound as exciting and positive an experience as we could. A nice lady was going to put her in a comfy chair and have a little look at her teeth, just to make sure everything was fine. There was absolutely nothing to worry about, and if she was a good girl we'd buy her some sweets on the way home. Vicki was fine about it, and was actually looking forward to this important rite of passage. But a few days beforehand she made the mistake of mentioning to someone at church that she was going to the dentist's. 'Oh no!' came back the response. 'I hope she doesn't hurt you! I had this root canal treatment, and . . .' In seconds all our hard work was undone.

That's how I remember evangelism from my youth. People were not interested, we were told, and they were so deep in sin and evil that you would have an almost impossible task in trying to 'convert' them. You would probably get persecuted into the bargain, perhaps in a way that involved physical violence. But just think what Jesus went through for you: if he endured being whipped, beaten and nailed to a cross, what was a bit of a kicking to worry about? The very way the narrative of personal evangelism was told made it seem like the scariest thing we'd ever have to do.

Another trait of some well-meaning Christians is the overwhelming urge to put people right. I could have had a field day with the lads: smoking, swearing, nicking stuff from the depot, quite apart from silly and misguided ideas about God: these were a normal part of everyday life. So when a vicar turned up for work the expectation of just about everyone there was that I would spend my whole time telling them off. Many of them told me that in so many words. Constantly putting people right with my superior theological knowledge might mean that I won the argument, but I'd most likely lose any further opportunities for discussion in the process, and that seemed too high a price to pay.

And then of course there is the really big one: words not backed up by lifestyle. Ask any non-Christian what Christians are like and they're bound to tell you sooner or later that we're a bunch of hypocrites. Again, the lads could tell me endless stories of people they knew who were supposed to be church-goers, but who had all sorts of things going on on the side, from fraud at work to playing away in their marriages. Nothing can set the cause of the gospel back more than Christians who lack integrity, or when words aren't backed up by actions.

Having to hear my mates' stories of counter-productive evangelism was a painful part of my upgrading, but I'm glad I did. I wish more Christians could hear some of them, which I suppose is why I've put this section in. I now knew what I had to avoid like the plague, and by all accounts I was beginning to do a half-decent job of it. But knowing what I shouldn't do was only half the story. What should I be doing instead?

This became much easier as I discovered the degree to which the guys did actually want to talk about God and faith.

With a flash of insight I realised that for them I had become a 'safe person'. In a world where faith is often privatised, and admission of any yearnings for something deeper in life can be seen as an admission of weakness, I had become someone to whom it was safe to talk. I wasn't going to harangue them, judge them, thump Bibles at them or ram anything down their throats. I would just listen, drop in the odd pertinent question and, if asked, give an account for the hope I have in me, with gentleness and respect. I realised that that famous verse from 1 Peter 3 did not actually say, 'Take every opportunity to twist conversations around to Jesus', as I had been brought up to believe.

I was indeed beginning to make a difference at IKEA, but when the end came it came quite suddenly. Literally one week before we were due to move out of our house, with still no prospect at all of where we might move to, I was offered a locum post in Jersey. In the space of a week we had booked a removal firm, packed up our house and were ready to start our next adventure.

10

A Year in Jersey

The year began with a migraine. We had watched as all our worldly goods, apart from those that we managed to pack into our two cars, had been put into huge crates and taken away for storage. Then we had driven to Portsmouth and said goodbye to the cars as they waited for loading onto the boat for the ten-hour crossing to St Helier. We had gone by train and were now waiting in Southampton airport for the short hop across to Jersey, when the familiar flickering in my eyes started, and I knew I was due for another attack. I tend to get migraines after I have been under stress, but once the stress has been resolved. I must be allergic to the sense of relief.

A helpful member of staff let me go and lie down in the sick room, and I set about my miracle cure for migraines, which fellow sufferers can have for nothing, if you haven't already discovered it. All you have to do is drink three pints of water straight down, and it will either abort the attack or severely limit it. I used to be out of action for between eight and twelve hours each time I got a migraine (thankfully not too often). Now I'm usually ready to go again in two to three. I feel as though I've been kicked in the head for a while, but I can usually function pretty well.

Eventually our flight took off, and I managed to survive the short hop across the water, landing in the November sunshine. We were to be met by one of the churchwardens of the parish we were going to for a short locum. Then we were taken to the vicarage, which was to be our home for the next three months (or so we thought). There was a huge sense of relief that we had finally escaped from the threat of homelessness, coupled with quite a bit of anxiety about how we'd fit in, in a couple of churches that hadn't really chosen us nor we them. This was purely a marriage of desperation. Later we were taken back to the docks to pick up our cars, which had survived the sea-crossing unscathed, and we set about unloading.

The house was amazing: we were about 50 yards from the seashore across a park, right in the centre of St Aubin's Bay, which forms much of the southern coast of the island. St Helier, the capital, was about a mile and a half along the coast to the east, and a similar distance in the opposite direction was the smaller town of St Aubin, which, as *Bergerac* fans will know, is the home of the Royal Courthouse pub, where Diamante Lil used to serve pints to her regulars. A coastal path/cycle track runs all around the bay, and at night coloured lights mark out this three mile arc. People from the two churches had clubbed together and found enough furniture for us to settle in happily, and the contents of our two cars completed the picture.

In spite of the idyllic setting, I had two great anxieties. One was having to take services, and the other was *where* I had to take services. After five years of itinerant ministry I had forgotten what it was like to be a normal vicar, taking services for the same bunch of people each week. And after three months of truck driving I had forgotten what it was like to take services at all. So I was dreading my first Sunday, which was approaching fast.

But even scarier was my venue. Those who have visited Jersey will almost certainly have heard of 'The Glass Church'. This was not, as I had assumed, some kind of a greenhouse: from the outside it looked very normal and unprepossessing. But the inside was a different matter. Florence Boot, widow of the famous chemists' magnate, had a villa in the South of France, and asked her neighbour, French glassmaker Réné Lalique, to fit out the interior of the local church of her other residence in Jersey in his inimitable style. So, apart from the wooden pews, just about everything else is made of Lalique glass. Lalique is best known for his small items: perfume bottles, vases, ornaments and so on, but in order to make the huge floor-to-ceiling panels with their characteristic Art Deco angels he had to invent a whole new recipe for his glass, a recipe that apparently died with him in 1945. This meant that the church was quite literally irreplaceable, and therefore truly priceless. My biggest fear was not that I'd preach a naff sermon or two, but rather that I would break something. This was no longer IKEA: I couldn't just get on the phone and order a new one. No pressure!

Well, my first Sunday came and went, the church remained intact, and people seemed to think I was OK. The parish of St Lawrence, in the centre of the island, had two churches: St Matthew's, the glass one, and the older parish church of St Lawrence, a mile or so inland. Each Sunday I had to take two services at St Lawrence, which was more rural and traditional, and then drive down the hill in order to get to St Matthew's as near the start of their service as I could. Then, in what I considered a very enlightened, Jersey kind of way, there were no evening services but rather cocktails *chez* the churchwardens. On very special occasions we would have champagne cocktails, but most of the time the normal ones had to do. I suppose that's slumming it Jersey-style.

Being a vicar is in some ways like riding a bike, and I quickly settled into parish life, discovering that I hadn't lost it after all. But the added advantage was that we all knew I was only there as a caretaker, and therefore it wasn't my place to go changing things. Inevitably we did make some minor tweaks, but it was wonderful not feeling the weight of responsibility to sort anything out. I was simply there to care for people, teach them and celebrate Communion for them.

One of my very first duties was to take the funeral service for the mother-in-law of one of the wardens. I had not had a chance to get to know her or the family that well, so I wasn't really prepared to turn up on the day and see Ian Hislop in the congregation. Ian was her nephew. I took a deep breath and carried on, and subsequently met Ian after the service, finding him to be every bit as charming and witty as he comes over on TV. I developed a great opening line, which I have saved up in my repertoire should I ever meet anyone else famous: 'Hello! I've seen you on the telly!' It seemed to strike the right chord between unfazed and sycophantic.

Although we had visited Jersey on a few occasions before, and had fallen in love with the place, we were a bit apprehensive about being there for more than just two weeks. All our friends from the mainland told us how claustrophobic it would feel after a while, and we had visions of a kind of Channel Islands cabin fever setting in, which might even result in us eating one another. In fact nothing could be further from the truth, and we settled quickly into the rhythms of island life. Vicki, now 7, was soon at home in her new school, and the boys were at university and on a gap year respectively. We loved the culture, the fact that secularisation has not set in as deeply as it has on the mainland, and the fact that, in spite of its problems, the island still retains a sense of politeness and respect. On one occasion I was walking the prom when a lad, complete with hoodie and baseball cap and on a skateboard, bumped into me. Picking himself up, he apologised profusely to me before wending his way onwards. I could just imagine that happening on the streets of Peckham.

We also loved the 'small island' mentality. Although there was one murder while we were there, which as you can imagine really rocked the whole place, the most exciting things to happen were usually more low-key. I can remember the screaming front-page banner headlines from the *Jersey Evening Post* one day: 'Car hits wall!' On another occasion I got a distressed phone call from my son, who was to leave his home on the mainland the next day for a stag weekend in Brussels. Did we know where his passport was? Indeed we did: it was in our filing cabinet in the vicarage. Explaining this dilemma to a friend, he had an idea: ring up Radio Jersey and ask if anyone was flying into East Midlands who could take Steve's passport and leave it at check-in. I'd never done anything like this before on Radio 1, but I was assured it would be fine. So I rang the radio station, explained my dilemma to a receptionist, and was asked to hold. Soon after I heard the DJ telling me 'Our next caller is John from St Lawrence. John – you're live on Radio Jersey: how can we help you?' I gulped, explained my problem to several thousand listeners, and in a few minutes I had a call back from a member of Flybe's cabin crew who said they would get Steve's passport to him that afternoon.

We had arrived on 5 November, so our first Christmas came upon us very quickly. It was also our silver wedding anniversary on Christmas Eve and, although some good friends came over for Christmas, we felt very isolated from our friends and family. So we decided instead to have open house. We made loads of cakes, bought plenty of cheap fizz (sadly not the real stuff from our special cocktail parties) and invited everyone from both churches to drop in during the day. This was an instant and immediate success. Not only did it bring people from the two churches together, but it also set the tone for our ministry. We have always tried to use our homes for hospitality. I reserve the right of clergy to use their homes as safe sanctuaries into which the life of the parish is never allowed to intrude, but that has not been our way. We found people coming into the vicarage for the first time ever, and taking the opportunity to have a good nose around. 'We'd always wondered what it was like inside!' we were told by many visitors.

The chance to celebrate a major family milestone with us meant that people quickly and easily took us to their hearts. The welcome we received was instant and heartfelt, and showed itself in a variety of practical ways. One parishioner turned up one day with his estate car absolutely brimming with logs for our open fire. Another family, on hearing me remark that my study was lovely but a bit dingy, gave me their account card for the local ironmonger's and told me I could spend 'say around £200 or so' on some new lighting. One farmer from St Lawrence kept us supplied with fresh veg, along with the occasional joint of some recently slaughtered animal. He used to bring milk for the after-service coffee: it was still warm from the cow, and was about half and half milk and thick cream.

There was a downside to being a rural rector: I had to bless things. More specifically I had to bless animals. A few times a year, on some obscure festivals that, as a townie, I had never really encountered before, the St Lawrence congregation would decamp to the churchwarden's farm, and I had to say prayers over some huge piece of livestock or other. Now don't get me wrong: I've got nothing against animals. Some of my best meals have contained them. But I much prefer to encounter them well done with pepper sauce than to get into a field with them and pray (although on the odd occasions in the past when I had found myself in a field of animals I certainly had prayed!). I tried telling Charles that my powers of blessing were so well developed that they could travel enough distance that I could do it from the safe side of the fence, but he would have none of it. Blessing was a hands-on business apparently. When I finally left the parish Charles, in his farewell speech, described me as all in all pretty good, but a bit of a wimp with the animals, an epithet of which I was in no way ashamed.

The weeks went by, and one of my greatest delights was to see the island emerge from its winter hibernation and become a holiday destination once again. As the evenings lengthened and the days became sunnier the little cafés that bordered the coastal walkway began to reopen. My first dip in the sea was on the Tuesday after Easter, although to be fair it nearly froze me to death. I've always loved spring the best of the four seasons, and to see not just flowers but the whole island coming to life was a real treat. As well as the spring blossom something else began to emerge at this time of year: hire cars. Because of the exorbitant cost of sea transport to the island (one company had the monopoly at the time, and could charge what they liked) most people flew over and hired cars. The vehicle population of the island almost doubles in the summer, and hire cars all have a red H on their number plates. Because driving in Jersey differs in some significant way from the mainland you have to watch out for 'H' cars and give them a wide berth. Whenever one cut us up or did something else wrong we would see the red H and tell each other 'He is an hireling and cannot be trusted!'

Another feature of life in the summer was that the boats came out. One Friday we had a call from some friends: were we free tomorrow, as they'd like to take us out to lunch? We were, and would love to, so we were told to meet them at St Helier marina at 12 noon. We expected lunch at the yacht club or something, but it turned out that we were going a bit further afield. Soon we were speeding towards France in their 36 ft cruiser, where we had a very passable lunch before sailing home again. We have subsequently had several holidays with the family, sleeping in luxury on the boat and pootling around the north coast of France.

Having successfully survived our first trip, Chris, who I have to say is not the world's best sailor, was very keen to accept another invitation from another couple for an overnight trip to France. But she didn't realise that their boat was a real yacht rather than a motor cruiser, and that therefore the motion was very different. You don't have to hang over the side in a powered boat, or mind your head when huge bits of wood and metal suddenly decide to swing round at you. Chris spent the entire crossing with her head in a bucket, felt ill all the time we were in France and knew that she would have to endure the journey home. Thus ended our sailing career.

Meanwhile, though, wonderful as Jersey life was, I still needed a job. The three months of my proposed locum came and went and, in spite of several applications and even a couple of interviews, I was no closer to permanent employment. To be fair I was not being hassled at all by the churches, who were between them paying my stipend out of their own resources. They had settled in to my being their vicar/rector, and we were all enjoying it. But I knew that the day of reckoning would come, not least because there were new moves afoot to appoint a permanent rector.

So the summer came, and I remember it as a long, hot, glorious one. Most days saw us spending at least some time on the beach: the only problem was choosing which beach we would visit on any given day. They varied so much in charac-ter, from little rocky coves on the north coast to the enormous five-mile sweep of St Ouen's, which forms the western edge of the island. Greve de Lecq had the best ice creams, Plemont the best digging and rock pools, and St Aubin's was just over the road. Decisions, decisions . . .

Far from finding the island claustrophobic we loved it, every inch of it, and I think we could happily have stayed on. In any case it was quick and easy to return to the mainland: in those days you could fly, if you picked the right time, for 99p each way. I had done a bit of lecturing on the mainland, and I used the visits to catch up with some friends. I also did get the occasional job interview, with expenses paid. But as the year passed idyllically by I could feel the panic rising up in me again, as I was still technically unemployed. In spite of the churches' generosity the cost of living was high, and we were also paying £50 per week for all the stuff we'd put into store, as well as our own pension contributions. My ministry was looking pretty successful, but my God was still silent.

The crunch came when the two parishes offered me the job on a permanent basis. We really agonised over that one. While on one level we would love to have stayed, there were other factors, which I won't bore you with now, that would have made it quite difficult. We finally reached the decision, graciously turned the job down, and continued on a locum basis. To this day we often regret that decision, particularly when it's cold and rainy.

Shortly after that someone, who interestingly was a friend of mine, was interviewed and appointed to the post. Once again we were on the move, but once again we had no job and nowhere to live. The sense of abandonment continued, and the fear grew as time ticked inexorably past. This download was really taking a long time!

11

Rescued Again!

The Jersey summer gave way to autumn, and just as we had enjoyed seeing the island wake up gradually during the spring, we now had to watch it shut down. The flowers died, the cafés were boarded up and the hirelings went home, making the roads safe once again. The sadness of this time was made worse as the arrival of the new vicar approached, and I still had nowhere to work or live on a permanent basis.

The only bright spark in this depressing time was the annual 'Tennerfest'. For a couple of weeks many of the hotels and restaurants would offer meals for a tenner or so, meals that had cost the hirelings much more during the summer. It was as though the catering trade was saying 'thank you' to the proper residents for putting up with all the tourists who had invaded their turf for six months. The art was to go to as many restaurants as you could afford during that two-week period, especially the ones that you could never afford to go to during the rest of the year. I think we did ourselves proud.

Then, once again just in the nick of time, we were offered another job. Although only a temporary one, there was the opportunity of a job-share with Chris looking after the children's ministry and me handling discipleship and training. Ever since she was a child Chris had wanted to work with children. She had, according to one of her old school books that we found, been through a phase of wanting to be a 'nuse' but she quickly realised that, with her aversions to both blood and sick, that might not be the best possible career choice. So as well as training as a teacher, she has throughout our ministry worked with children and teenagers, with phenomenal gifting and great success. This job-share allowed her to continue this passion, driven for her by an awareness that so often we short-change our churches' children by giving them the crumbs of resourcing and spirituality from the richly laden table of the adults. Children are so often the poor and voiceless ones in the life of the church, and Chris has always made it her role to put into their young lives the very best in terms of quality, resources and spiritual expectations. Another church on the island could finance us on a short-term basis, and there was even somewhere to live, albeit much less grand than the vicarage, so we could both continue our different ministries, at least for a while longer. With a sigh of relief we packed up and moved again, although over the year we had accumulated so much stuff that our cars would no longer do the job. Downsizing was a scary prospect, but was offset by one important factor: we were to have an Aga. We'd never had one before, and probably will never again, but for a while this was a dream come true.

Our careers at our new church began with a staff lunch, at which I distinguished myself greatly. I had wanted to make an impact, and I certainly did. There was a bottle of salad cream on the table and, as is my habit, I picked it up and gave it a good shake, only to find that the top came off. I created a beautiful arc of white goo that spread from the table onto the ceiling, the far wall, the settee and the carpet of the vicarage. They were beautifully kind to me, but my desire to make an entrance to my new job made a lot of cleaning up necessary.

We settled in quickly to our new roles. We had known the church for some years: in fact the first time we ever visited Jersey was at their invitation, and we had become good friends with the vicar and his family. The change from rural ministry, where basically I did most of it, to being in an urban church with a large staff team took a while, but we felt once again that we were among friends and that our ministry was valued. Christmas came and went, with still no prospect of permanent employment, and before long we were beginning to watch the island wake from its winter slumber for the second time. We couldn't help but wonder whether we'd get a second Tennerfest too. But this time there was a definite end point. The house we were living in was a holiday rent owned by a local Methodist minister, but he had his first summer booking from the beginning of May. It was non-negotiable that we would have to be out before then, and as the weeks passed into months the spectre of homelessness began to haunt us again.

Because Chris and I were job-sharing I had some time to myself, which I thought I might as well use profitably. I did this in two ways, taking funerals and setting up a little business teaching people how to use computers. The funeral bit was easy: I've already mentioned how much I enjoy this ministry, and I soon got in with the island funeral directors and was kept pretty busy. I know that many parish priests resent 'freelancing' by retired clergy, but I found rather that many were only too glad of the help. And because I made it a policy that I would liaise with them, so that ongoing pastoral care for the family was possible, I found nothing in the way of resentment.

But Jersey funerals have some significant differences, as is the case in many regions of the country. The main thing is the after service line-up. It is the custom that the immediate family wait in the porch at the church or crematorium and shake hands with everyone who has been at the service. The minister then stands at the end of the line. So it has something of the feel of going into a wedding reception, but without the Buck's Fizz. This was fine once I'd got used to it, but as you can imagine for larger services it could add a considerable amount of time. One funeral I took was that of a well-known and popular sailor: there must have been close on 300 people crammed into the chapel. Leaving the service took far longer than the service itself had done, and I had booked myself another appointment, for which I was a good forty-five minutes late. I learnt my lesson after that.

There is also some interesting theology around at funerals, but none more worrying than that of one family I visited who were convinced beyond any doubt that their deceased granny had now turned into a seagull. I felt incredibly guilty about this, and desperately hoped that granny hadn't been the seagull at whom I had lobbed a stone only the day before on the beach when it tried to swoop down and nick my chips.

The computer business was much more fun, and I soon picked up a small client base, mainly of retired people from around the island church community, who were using their third age to explore the wonders of e-mail, the internet and so on. I love teaching anyone anything, and the bit of pin money I made helped me as I hope I helped my punters.

Our year and a half in Jersey was drawing to a close, with still no idea where we would be going to next. I think of all the places we have lived we would still regard Jersey as the closest we have found to feeling like a home, and we felt incredibly loved and valued by the people there. We have never known such generosity and such a welcome. Were it not for the fact that we are not millionaires, we would gladly return there for our retirement, but alas they have strict regulations about who can live on the island. Unless you were born there, marry someone from there or meet one of the other various 'quallies' or qualifications, the only way is to buy a property worth over £1 million. So it might have to be Sheffield instead: a lovely city, but the beaches are nowhere near as good. Indeed they're nowhere near.

So life went on, and we enjoyed our different areas of ministry, but still had no plans for the future other than homelessness, and no idea why God should be so cruel as to unplug his phone and refuse to answer our calls. I often tell people that if you have to go through a wilderness experience, Jersey isn't a bad place to do it, but beneath the great life we were leading and the warm welcome and good friends, we were empty and hopeless inside. My greatest regret is that this spell on a paradise island was such that I could never really enjoy it. All the time we were coping with the silence and absence of God, tremendous fear for the future and a real lack of purpose and direction in our lives. If I could have that time over again I hope that I would learn to relax into it and enjoy it more, and to trust God for the future. But at the time I found it impossible, and lived what was actually a highly privileged life against the background hum of fear, anxiety and abandonment, like a nagging toothache that spoils everything else.

So what was God downloading into me during that time? One particular Bible passage became important to me – John 6:60–68. Jesus was finding that in some circles at least he was no longer flavour of the month, and people were deserting him in their droves. Finally he turned to his disciples, his closest friends, and asked them, 'You do not want to leave too, do you?'

Peter replied (and this is my translation of the text): 'Yes, Lord, I'd love to, but unfortunately we've got no-one else to go to. After all, you do have the words of eternal life. So I suppose we'd better stick around.'

I'm not sure if that is what Peter actually said or meant, but that idea, that while it would be tempting to walk away, there would be absolutely nowhere else to go, became really significant for me. On one level I could see no earthly reason for continuing to live the Christian life, or to serve this God who had so thoroughly abandoned me. But what else could I do? I believed this stuff was true; I'd given my life for it, and for trying to communicate it to other people, so what else did I have to provide my life with any meaning at all? Even if I could have stayed on as a truck driver or computer trainer, that hardly seemed to me to be a purposeful existence or a good use of my gifts.

I had some really big questions about God's last-minute way of doing things too. Psalm 37:25 tells me that, 'I was young and now I am old, yet I have never seen the righteous forsaken or their children begging bread.' Leaving aside the difficult question of Christians in areas of the world where that is exactly what they have to do, I would say without doubt that my testimony agrees with that. As a family we have come very close to the edge on a number of occasions, but we have always seen God provide for us. But why oh why does he so often leave it to the very last minute? And why do I seem to be incapable of using the evidence from the past to trust him for the future? People talk blithely about God 'testing' us: if that is what's going on all I can say is that I have consistently failed the test.

This existential crisis was made even worse by the fact that I am what you would call a 'charismatic'. Not for me some deist god who remains uninterested and uninvolved in human life, watching from a distance. I had a God who did speak, who did answer prayers, who did act in the lives of his people – or at least who *used* to do those things. I have no trouble at all with the 'interventionist' God who is so sneered at in some church circles, because my Bible tells me about a thoroughly interventionist God. But that belief does make it ten times worse when he decides not to intervene as I would like him to.

A while after I left IKEA and Jersey I had the chance to write a book about my experiences of abandonment. It was a joint title, with a friend who would also proudly call himself charismatic and had recently watched his wife die painfully of MS.[17] I have to admit that, beside his, my problems seemed insignificant, but that didn't make life any less painful for me. But as we talked and reflected together I was gradually able to make some sense of this experience of abandonment. I came to understand the nature of the upgrade God was offering me. It was all about steadfastness and endurance.

These virtues are mentioned often in the Bible as very positive things to cultivate. God himself is of course the ultimate in reliability. He never changes, is called our 'rock', can be trusted without question and endures for ever. But more interesting are the biblical calls for us to be as steadfast as he is. The psalms contain many prayers for, as well as protestations of, steadfastness. 'Create in me a pure heart, O God, and renew a steadfast spirit within me' cries the penitent psalmist in Psalm 51:10. 'Oh, that my ways were steadfast in obeying your decrees!' longs Psalm 119:5. Isaiah promises that God 'will keep in perfect peace those whose minds are steadfast, because they trust in you' (Isa. 26:3), a truth that I so totally failed to grasp during this time. In the New Testament steadfastness and endurance are both promised and commanded. Paul's parting exhortation at the very end of his first Corinthian letter is typical: 'Therefore, my dear brothers and sisters, stand firm. Let nothing move you. Always give yourselves fully to the work of the Lord, because you know that your labour in the Lord is not in vain' (1 Cor. 15:58). We are to resist the devil's attacks 'steadfast in the faith', we are to endure hardship and, above all, we are to persevere, never giving up or losing the plot. When life, or other people, turns against us, we are to hang in there.

In fact the Bible is full of material about endurance, steadfastness, perseverance and the rest. But it's true to say that I can't remember ever hearing a single talk about it. Sadly I can't remember ever preaching one either, at least not until this latest upgrade (now I bang on about it all the time!). I think there are two main factors to blame for this tragic lack.

The first is the comfortable consumerism that is the culture in which we live. There's a line in the Anglican Communion service that talks about it being 'our duty and our joy' to praise and thank God. I reckon we've got this a bit out of balance: if it doesn't feel like joy, we're not that bothered about it. My parents' generation had a highly developed sense of duty: it's what made them count it a privilege to serve their country in warfare, to be loyal and good citizens, to be hard and diligent workers and to serve the church tirelessly. It's what made them sit week in week out through what I might have considered mind-numbingly boring Prayer Book services without a single hint of life to them: they were doing their duty to God by being there. One might wish for a bit more joy for that generation, but that's nothing to the rediscovery of duty that the next one needs. What a different world my kids inhabit!

So why on earth endure? If something doesn't seem to be working, or isn't going well, why on earth stick with it? If I'm not getting happiness, or fulfilment, or satisfaction, or any other of the other prizes that our culture says we can't live without, why on earth not just give up and do something different? This way of thinking has permeated the church as much as it has permeated society, and so sermons about the virtues of flogging what appear to be dead horses are quite understandably not flavour of the month.

The second factor, I believe, is that we have adopted far too readily a model of church as 'happy family'. There are several different pictures in the Bible of the company of God's people, both pre- and post-cross: things such as pilgrims, priesthood, nation, bride, army, body – you name it. My default model for church has always been the army of God. I find this a purposeful, dynamic model: we have a calling, a mission, battles to fight, people to rescue, victories to win, which mean that we need training, fitness, discipline and obedience. Yet again and again I hear churches self-defining as 'the church family', a model that lacks any purpose, does not have any growth imperative (in fact families often take deliberate steps to ensure that they don't grow any bigger) and is much more about being than doing, about comfort than sacrifice. I also note with interest that you have to look pretty hard in Scripture to find any mention of church as family. We have replaced the camaraderie forged in battle for the comfy security of family life, where we are happy to welcome those we choose to let in because they are like us. So once again terms like 'endurance' simply don't seem relevant to this happy, comfortable gathering. This was an insight that was later to get me into big trouble, but more of that later.

Of course no one biblical picture of the church will cover all the bases: that's why there are so many different ones. But I believe that an over-emphasis on church as family will militate against any need for the kind of spiritual fitness and discipline implied in words like 'steadfastness'.

So I have come to believe that God was using this desperately difficult period of my life to download into me those kinds of qualities that he must have thought of as lacking up to that point. In fact there was little choice about it: I genuinely did have nowhere else to go, and I genuinely did believe that he and he alone had the words of eternal life. But since then I think I have developed a much greater awareness of the need simply to hang in there and just get on with the job. And I believe I'm the richer for it.

I was running a training day on prayer ministry at a neighbouring church when the phone call came through. I had been for yet another interview, this time for the post of Parish Development Advisor in the Welsh Diocese of Monmouth. I had little knowledge of the church in Wales, but I liked the sound of the job, so I was desperate enough to have a stab. Much to my delight I was called for interview, and the next day the bishop rang to offer the post to me. At last two years of unemployment were over. I had landed a proper, permanent job again, with a real house to live in!

12

Land of My Fathers

Once again we packed up our life, or as much of it as we could get into our cars, and set off on the ferry to Poole – and then on to South Wales. I don't think I've ever felt as deep a sadness as I felt watching the island disappear gradually behind us. Even though I was excited about my new role, and relieved that it was at last a permanent one, I was devastated to be leaving the place that had become for us the closest thing to home. Somehow our two cars became separated at the docks, so the drive to Newport was a solitary one. We met up at the house, and found once again that in spite of all the warning, the builders were still in and it wasn't ready for us. It was all we could do not to turn around and head back to Poole, but we bravely camped out until the work was finished and our furniture arrived in two lots, one from storage in Derby and one from Jersey. It wasn't a good start.

Having lived in Jersey we thought we understood cross-cultural ministry. Jersey had been like England but a bit different around the edges, and we had every expectation that Wales would be the same. In fact we were going to just about the most English bit of Wales. Monmouthshire had changed sides a few times during its history, but just happened to be in Wales at the moment. Hardly anyone at all spoke Welsh as their first language, and precious few spoke it at all. We were sure we'd fit in fine. But we were in for a big shock: even in Monmouthshire and Gwent we were most definitely in a foreign land, a land where at best the English were treated with suspicion by many, and downright hostility by a few.

My role was Parish Development Advisor for the Diocese of Monmouth, which I defined as promoting anything that would lead to life, health and growth in the churches of the diocese. I was a member of the senior staff of the diocese, under Bishop Dominic Walker, and I also carried the portfolio for Stewardship. Inevitably I picked up some liturgical responsibilities too, which was useful as the all-new Welsh Communion liturgy was launched in 2004 while I was there, the first permanent modern-language service. I soon became a member of 'Governing Body', the Welsh equivalent of General Synod and, wearing my Stewardship hat, I worked with advisors from the other five dioceses, as well as with the C of E networks. Fairly soon, as has always been my lot, my teaching skills were recognised and I was used across the province to do some teaching and training.

But within the diocese I got a mixed reception, it would be fair to say. There is an interesting relationship between parish clergy and the 'hierarchy' or the diocesan officers. There is a common view that, while bishops can occasionally be useful, the real ministry takes place on the coal face of parish life, and bureaucrats who sit on their backsides in the diocesan office are a waste of time and money. In spite of the fact that the entire diocese was run by a team of seven people working in the office, who between them handled all the finance, publicity, buildings, personnel and so on, we were clearly resented by some in the churches. I had of course joined in with this thinking in the past: now I was to see it from the other side. But I seemed especially prone to animosity as mine was a new post, created by the bishop after a successful model used in his previous diocese.

The senior staff team was a great group to belong to. The bishop and the two archdeacons, along with myself, the diocesan secretary, the communications officer and latterly the training officer made up the team, and we had such fun together. Being a member of this team, and working much more closely than ever before with the bishop, gave me real insight into the issues of running a diocese, and the sheer number of plates a bishop has to keep spinning. We worked hard, but we played hard as well and, thanks to his enormous generosity, the bishop would often stand us meals together, which were great social and team-building events. On one memorable occasion one of the archdeacons pushed the boat out and chose kangaroo steak from the menu, earning him the nickname 'Skippy' from then on.

It was a real inspiration working under Bishop Dominic. As a monk, a member of a religious community, he had developed over the years a deep discipline of prayer and reflection on the Scriptures. On one occasion someone was going on about how we needed to pray more: Dominic let slip that he spent two hours in prayer every morning before we met for our 8 a.m. Eucharist. He was also deeply wise, unflappable and had a passion to see the churches in his diocese thrive and grow. He was incredibly generous: he had a wine cellar of some repute and, when he invited us round, as he often did, he showed himself to be an excellent cook, especially of his favourite Italian foods. Apparently some wag had once referred to him as 'an opulent ascetic': someone else, on seeing his 'palace', remarked, 'If this is poverty, I wouldn't like to see his chastity!'

Purely on financial grounds his 'company car' was a shiny black Mercedes. This was a choice based on the fact that in order to be seen to be saving money one of his fellow bishops had chosen a Skoda. Cheap to buy, but when the time came to trade it in it was worth virtually nothing. Dominic did his research and discovered that the resale value of a Merc after five years was so high that all in all it would save the church thousands. He was an IAM member, and was very proud of his lovely car. On one occasion, taking a confirmation service in a run-down part of Newport Docks, he asked the vicar if his car would be safe parked on the road. 'Perfectly safe,' came the reply. 'The only people around here who drive Mercs are the drug dealers, and no-one dares mess with their motors!'

Dominic was also an excellent teacher. One Lent he decided, with our encouragement, to clear his diary and do a speaking tour, expounding some themes from St John's gospel Monday to Friday in five centres around the diocese for the six weeks of Lent. It is never easy getting people to turn out to things in the church, but this was a sell-out: some of the venues were standing room only, and around a thousand people came to hear him, and kept coming week by week. I reflected that it is a shame that so often bishops are so busy with admin and discipline matters that they just do not have time to teach, which is one of their original roles. The tour was a roaring success and, in spite of the punishing schedule, Dominic loved it too.

Working as a member of senior staff was a bit like going back to being a curate again and, as I had been with Robert Warren all those years ago in Sheffield, I found myself being formed and shaped in the presence of such a deeply Spirit-filled servant of God. So much of what God downloads into us comes from those with whom we rub shoulders: I was certainly inspired by working with such a wise and deep person.

A while into the job Chris and I were sent by Dominic on a short course called 'Welcome to Wales', designed by '*Cytun*' (Welsh 'Churches Together') for those moving into ministry in Wales and seeking to understand the background and culture within which they would be ministering. As well as fascinating outings like a trip to the Welsh Assembly Government in Cardiff Bay, we were taught about the history and background of the Welsh church. I began to get an insight into the tensions between the Welsh and the English, and also began to understand the nature of Welsh Christianity. So much of it was about the Welsh language.

In an attempt to keep the Welsh language alive, a very commendable notion, it was the law that all children had to learn Welsh up to GCSE level. So Vicki had to begin from scratch at the age of 9, but very quickly emerged as top of the class. All signs in Wales had to be bilingual too. So even the 'bus stop' on the tarmac in lay-bys was accompanied by '*safle bws*', in case the bus driver couldn't understand English. We had a very amusing day at Governing Body debating a motion that the Church in Wales had to be fully bilingual, right down to the way the phone was answered in each diocesan office. This would have presented a real dilemma in our diocese, as no-one who worked in the office could speak any Welsh, and indeed it was almost impossible in Newport to find anyone who could. The motion was duly passed, but with the proviso that it only applied where appropriate. A great relief to Monmouth, but also a complete waste of a day.

Many years ago at school I had started to learn Welsh, just for a laugh really, but my language learning skills, never that sharply honed, had almost totally deserted me. Anyway, I was assured, I just would not need Welsh in Monmouth Diocese. I think there were maybe two churches in the whole diocese where any Welsh was spoken in worship. Eventually I did manage to learn the blessing at the end of the service, but I only ever used it once in earnest, and that was while I was on holiday in Florida ministering at a friend's church. I figured that very few people in the USA would know whether I'd got it right or not, but that it would give them something to remember. But now, on the course, I was discovering just what potent things nationalism and language were.

We heard how English had been imposed on Welsh speakers. Partly it was about safety: when there was an influx of English and Canadian workers into the mines, there had to be a quick and easy way of communicating 'Get out – now!', so English became the standard language. We heard about the piece of rope with a knot that was placed around the neck of any child who let slip a Welsh word in schools: whoever was wearing the rope at the end of school got a beating. I have no doubt that the Welsh were treated appallingly badly by the English at different points in history, and we deserve any animosity that we may experience as visitors.[18] But the thing I found most sad was that even in the Christian community no-one seemed capable of forgiving, forgetting and moving on. Even at this Christian conference I experienced that familiar scenario of an English person coming into the room and everyone suddenly switching to Welsh. If the Christian church cannot find the resources to forgive and move on, what hope is there for the nations at large?

It was also language that led to the fragmentation of non-conformity in Wales. In a small town, visited by John Wesley, a Methodist chapel might be started. But there was then the need for a Welsh-speaking Methodist chapel and an English-speaking Methodist chapel. Then when the inevitable splits happened between the Wesleyan Methodists and some other brands, the effects were to be doubled. Sometimes English people moved in, and there an English Methodist church was started. Some of the incomers might begin to learn Welsh out of love for their new culture, so then there was a Welsh-speaking English Methodist church. Multiply that by several other free-church denominations, and you can see why there are so many carpet warehouses in disused chapels around Wales.

The Welsh language was not without its amusement, though. At Governing Body, which met a couple of times each year for a residential session, each diocese took it in turns to produce and lead the worship, and when it was Monmouth's turn I got the job, as the nearest thing we had to a resident liturgist. Of course everything had to be bilingual: each two-page spread would have Welsh on one side and English on the other. Surprisingly very little Welsh liturgy is available on-line, so I had painstakingly to type out huge swathes of text from the book, letter by letter and accent by accent, without a clue what it meant or whether I had typed it correctly. As you can imagine, the page was filled with squiggly red underlining. Then I had a brainwave: minority language though it was, could it be the case that Microsoft had produced a Welsh add-on spell-checker? I searched online and to my delight found one. I downloaded and installed it, ran the checker, and lo and behold every single red line disappeared, including those under words that it later transpired I had spelt incorrectly. I could just imagine Bill Gates issuing instructions to some geek in his company, 'Just bung in a bit of code that says "remove all red lines" and market it as a Welsh spell-checker. Who's going to know?'

My other favourite Welsh story, apparently true, was of a young English woman who had moved with her husband to Wales, and fallen in love with the country, the culture and the language, even though she couldn't speak a word of it. When she had her first baby she was determined to give it a lovely Welsh-sounding name, so, looking around the hospital ward after the birth for inspiration, she decided to go for 'Allanfa Dân' because it sounded beautifully Welsh and had that tantalising circumflex accent for a bit of distinction. So her daughter in due time was christened Allanfa Dân, which, when being translated, means 'Fire Exit'.

It would be an exaggeration to say that in Wales the Reformation has not yet happened, but it was a surprise to us that the Church in Wales (the Welsh Anglican Church) is almost unremittingly catholic in flavour, not just in worship style but also in attitude. It was a useful learning experience for me to discover the intricacies of catholic worship; how many times to swing the incense at this point, and where I needed to drop to one knee. I also discovered that what 'Father' says goes: the clergy have virtually all the power, and the people 'know their place'. Yet, in spite of the culture shock for a good Baptist boy, I discovered underneath it all a deep spirituality, and a desire, or at least a stated desire, for growth and new life. But as I tried to spread the gospel of new ways of doing church, I discovered something that I have since found to be equally true this side of Offa's Dyke: people just don't get it.

I found again and again that while people said they wanted growth and change, there were so many no-go areas of tradition that it was almost impossible to conceive of the idea of doing anything new or different. As I was not attached to a church, we made our home in a fairly local parish that was even more Anglo-Catholic than most. The vicar was a good preacher, the music was excellent and the liturgy well done, even if we had to cross our fingers behind our backs at some bits of it. After a while I was asked to lead an Alpha course, to which over fifty of the congregation came. They loved it! Everything went really well until week ten when we had to think about the church. I used my talk to share the insight from my IKEA days that most of what goes on in church buildings on a Sunday morning is totally irrelevant to the vast majority of people 'out there', and that we had to think hard about new ways of being and doing church. This went down like a crocodile in a swimming pool, and it was made very clear after that that I was *persona non grata* at that church.

The line was that once people experience the riches of the catholic faith they'll want to come to church, and how dare I suggest that their style was in any way inadequate? In my travels around the diocese I discovered that this attitude was rife. This triumph of naivety over statistical fact seemed to me like a death-wish. I was reminded of Jesus' words over the doomed city of Jerusalem: 'If you, even you, had only known on this day what would bring you peace – but now it is hidden from your eyes' (Luke 19:42). Like Jesus I was often on the receiving end of personal animosity for daring to question or suggest that current church life might not be totally working.

Leaving that church, we joined another where I was to learn, to my shame, the truth that when we point one finger at someone else we point three back at ourselves. I had been asked by Dominic to look after a young priest who had been brought into the diocese to pioneer some new work, based in an interesting church that, through the determination and sheer hard work of a small number of faithful people, had not just avoided closure but re-ordered their church building. Right in the main drag of Newport, it boasted a café, meeting rooms and a highly flexible worship space. While we got on really well with the new guy and his family (and still do), I was amazed to find myself quite critical of some elements of his style. He hated dressing up for worship, and would much rather lead worship in tatty jeans and trainers. His preferred musical style was mainly based around charismatic worship songs, which, after the rich diet of liturgical music in our previous church, seemed bland and a bit boring. He was a real entrepreneur, and decided to nag the diocese until they let him have an unused vicarage on one of the worst estates in the city to house a community of students who would engage in outreach work in local schools. Much to my surprise I found myself reacting strongly against all these new ideas: that just wasn't how you did church! It took me some time to see the irony: I was as conservative, as set in my ways, as traditional, as the churches I was working with. It was just that the line in the sand was in a different place. As I write, that church is thriving and growing, they are looking to set up a second house community and they are probably the most successful church in the diocese. God had to download into me an awareness not just of the traditionalism of the church but also my own, and I am sadder and wiser because of it.

What else was God working into me at this time? The main thing, I think, was that he was preparing me for perhaps the greatest shock of my career, which was shortly to come and hit me. When working with churches and their leaders I found myself often impatient at the clergy for what I perceived as their weakness in the face of opposition from powerful lay people. Often I would sit with clergy who would wring their hands and say things like 'Yes, I can see that that would be a great idea, and would help us grow, but my PCC simply would not allow it.' I found it perplexing and frustrating that, in a catholic culture where 'Father' wielded such authority, clergy were still so afraid of and hampered by their flocks. I was soon to have plenty of time to repent of this attitude.

My time in Wales did bring one unexpected delight: my first venture into the world of film. Dominic had asked me to write a Lent course for use in the diocese, and my son Paul, who after not one but three gap years was preparing to go to university to do a degree in Moving Image Design, urged me to consider making a DVD as well as writing a booklet. I used some of the insights I had gained on evangelism from my time at IKEA, and we produced a course called *Safe Evangelism – Sharing your faith so it doesn't hurt*. It received a good reaction from the diocese (although I'm not sure how much long-term effect it had) but the making of it was such fun. The diocese paid Paul to be cameraman, editor, special effects department and director, and we went far and wide searching for the right locations to film the material. The inevitable out-takes form an articulate commentary on the fun we had, as well as on our incompetence as film-makers, but we had got the bug, and *Safe Evangelism* was followed up with an instructional DVD on *Mission Action Planning* for the diocese.

The time to leave Wales came on purely pragmatic grounds. There were no dramatic calls or voices this time, no prophetic words and not even a small angel. It just seemed like common sense. I had done five years, and Vicki was about to begin her GCSE courses. If we didn't move now, it would be at least two, if not four, years until the next window. By that stage I would be over 60 and almost unemployable, so it seemed right to make the break now while I still had a good ten or eleven years left in me. It was also a policy decision to go back to parish ministry, after ten years in more specialist minis- try. Although Chris had managed to continue her minis- try among children and young people in the churches we attended, she had no official role in the diocese, and we both felt that a return to parish ministry would once again allow us to minister as we preferred, as a couple. We began looking for jobs, and eventually I was appointed to the parish that, for reasons that will become apparent, I will call St Basil's, which was not really in deepest Dorset.

13

Pride and a Fall

I arrived at St Basil's confident of a successful ministry. Chris and I had carefully read the parish profile (a document prepared by the church council to give factual information about the church, the parish and the area, and also to 'sell' the job of vicar), and had an increasing sense that this partnership could work. They told us they were a proudly evangelical church that contained people from across the evangelical spectrum from conservative to charismatic and all stations between. They had a great record of social-action projects, and much involvement in a deprived area of Dorset, even though the parish itself was a lot more middle class than those around it. There was a large paid staff and a significant team for me to lead. Of course they wanted to grow and to reach out more successfully into the parish. Clearly I was just what they needed!

After all, I ruminated, every parish I had worked in had seen numerical growth and renewal; I had spent ten years teaching others how to lead vibrant parishes; and now for my final job I was going back to the coal face to make it all work for myself one last time. As we say while we're watching *Casualty* on telly: what could possibly go wrong?

In fact, it was a disaster. This chapter isn't easy for me to write, partly because it is still raw and partly because it shows me up in a bad light. It would have been easy to miss this bit of my life and learning out, but I have since discovered that what I was to experience at St Basil's is not at all rare, yet no-one really talks about it unless they've been through it themselves. It has also provided one of the biggest and most significant downloads of my life so far, so to ignore it would leave a huge gap in the story. Just allow me to remind you that the church wasn't called St Basil's; I have disguised this part of the story. Neither is it anywhere near Dorset. But the essence of it is true, although of course I can only write from my point of view: others would recount the story from theirs. The bottom line is that four years after I arrived, I was to leave the parish, broken and bruised. For the first time in my career I experienced a failed ministry.

I won't give you the blow-by-blow account, but the demise of my ministry centred, I think, around three things: ecclesiology, theology and missiology. In other words, we were to fall out over what kind of church we thought we were, what we believed the Bible said church ought to be like, and how we were to see people come to faith and discipleship. Apart from those three areas, everything else was fine!

The first thing I discovered was that St Basil's sat lightly to its Anglicanism. Like many evangelical churches, they didn't really 'get' or enjoy liturgical worship. They used it, of course, just, but without flair or creativity. Worship was all about words, and my attempts to engage other senses were treated with suspicion. One of the options in my inaugural licensing service was to sprinkle the congregation with water to remind them of their baptism: this is usually a good-natured bit of fun, but when I did it I was marked as 'high church'. My attempts to renew the liturgy, to add a bit of colour and variety, and to take seriously the different seasons of the church year, were seen as further evidence of my catholic tendencies. As a result, people started to leave the church.

I was saddened to realise that questions of churchmanship and style were so powerful, and I felt misunderstood: not by the wildest stretch of imagination could I be described as an 'anglo-catholic', even though I had spent some time in those circles.

I should mention that part of the deal if you're an Anglican church is the certain amount of bureaucracy it entails. One aspect of this is the legal requirement to keep accurate week-by-week attendance records. When I looked for these figures I found the relevant column in the service register empty as far back as I could go. This might seem an unimportant piece of paperwork, but it was to come back and bite me later. I made sure that from my first Sunday onwards accurate records were kept.

This churchmanship issue was a relatively minor niggle, but like a tiny stone in your shoe it continued to cause irritation throughout my ministry. But the question of what sort of church we were loomed larger as time went by. I was beginning to find that in spite of calling themselves an evangelical church, there were some significant gaps. First of all I tried to gather people for a monthly prayer meeting, which we called 'PowerHouse', since, as we all knew, prayer is indeed the powerhouse of any enterprise for the kingdom. But out of a membership of around 250 people, we struggled to get 20 to meet to pray for an hour a month. Secondly, in spite of my attempts to run Alpha courses, which I had found to be so successful in the past, only two people from the church ever invited anyone along. Alpha simply didn't work in this setting. And then my attempts to include more Bible in our worship, with the inclusion of at least two readings, plus an occasional psalm, were seen to be further evidence of my anglo-catholic leanings. On a bad day I felt as though I were leading an evangelical church that didn't gather to pray, didn't do evangelism and didn't seem to like the Bible much.

I also tried to provide training for various elements of Christian service. I offered a course on prayer ministry: one person signed up. I offered regular training and support for homegroup leaders: only a proportion of them opted in. My suggestion that homegroups ought to grow and multiply was treated as though it were a sad joke, and in fact most of my preaching and teaching appeared to fall on deaf ears. Immensely frustrated, I came to realise two important things: I had come in proudly assuming that I could lead St Basil's into growth, but instead we were declining fast. And I was trying to import elements that had worked in the past elsewhere, but they just weren't working here.

I can remember my vicar from my Sheffield days, Robert Warren, recounting his experience of renewal coming when he came to the point of realizing that, like the man in Jesus' parable in Luke 11, he had 'nothing to set before them'. He had reached the end of his own resources and felt broken and helpless, with no idea what to do next. I felt this same sense of powerlessness even to dent the culture of the church I believed God had called me to, but the outcome was not as happy as Robert's turned out to be.

About two years in, we experienced something pretty rare in Anglican circles, but common elsewhere: a church split. This happened when a member of staff left and took many of the congregation with her. I won't go into the details, but suffice it to say that the drawn-out battle that culminated in their departure left me even more exhausted and discouraged. I felt, however, that at least with the presenting issues now out into the open and dealt with, we could go on and grow. But lurking underneath was a fundamental disagreement about the theology of church.

At one PCC meeting a discussion arose about 'the church family'. This common term, which may sound comfortable and cosy, is actually one I have long avoided (and have explained why in a previous chapter). But what became clear during the discussion was that, while I have always worked with the model of church as 'army', St Basil's self-defined as a 'happy family'. We were thus suffering from a fundamental mismatch of expectations, and in a flash of inspiration I could see why I was feeling so frustrated. If you're leading an army you have a bunch of people on a mission, with purpose to live for, an enemy to overcome, people to rescue and so on. Therefore what people need is training, fitness, discipline, equipping . . . you get the idea. But if you're living as a happy family you don't need any of these things. Instead you look for hugs, affirmation and someone nice to bring you flowers when you go through hard times. I caricature, but I suddenly realised that I was working on an agenda in which most people had no interest. That explained why my attempts to mobilise prayer, evangelism and training had been treated with apathy. Usually my answer to just about anything is to pray about it and to teach into it. I'm with Paul, who, when countering error in his churches would declare in frustration 'Don't you *know* . . . ?' (see Romans 6:16; 11:2; 1 Corinthians 3:16; 5:6; 9:13). If only people knew they would be fine, so roll in the teachers and put them straight. I decided that we needed a teaching series on 'Biblical pictures of church'. Of course I knew that one biblical model had no monopoly, even that of the army, and so I thought it would be helpful if we could look at several different models and assess the positive and negative aspects of each.

But the teaching didn't connect. As one member of the council later articulated on behalf of the church: 'We don't want to be an army: we want to be a family!' My frustration only increased with my sense of powerlessness. It felt just like the experience of trying to remove an intransigent bolt whilst fitting new suspension onto my car: it was as though I had used up all the tools I had in my toolkit, and nothing had shifted by even a millimetre. I just did not know what else to do. Clearly my approach to ministry was failing to win people over. If ever I needed an upgrade it was now, but nothing came to rescue me. I think that was the moment I realised that I would have to leave, but let me come to that part of the story in a moment.

So ecclesiologically I was too Anglican, and theologically I was working on a different model of church. That just left mission, and this was to be the area that would see me come unstuck altogether. Almost by accident we had started a new early service on Sunday mornings that was far more informal, attracting people of all ages but primarily the young families who were missing from the rest of the church. The service grew slowly, but was treated with suspicion by some from the later congregation, which was still declining in numbers. This service provided the battlefield for my final defeat when some people decided it should be folded back into the mainstream. They said it was destroying the 'family' unity of the church, in spite of us already having a church plant that met at the same time as our new service but in a different venue. I failed to understand the logic of this, but battle had been joined and logic seemed to go out of the window.

Thus, three years into my ministry, I was asked for my resignation. I was told that this was in accordance with the wishes of 80 per cent of the congregation. Along with a list of my personal failings, it was claimed that numbers were still declining, although of course since no records had been kept from before my arrival any 'evidence' was anecdotal. As far as any of us knew, St Basil's might have been in long, slow decline, perhaps for decades. That was certainly true of our ministry to children: in spite of photos from an era forty years in the past showing a thriving children's ministry, by the time we arrived we had about six on the books, which meant that any given week we might get two.

Things came to a head six months later at a fateful church council meeting. By then we had turned the corner and begun to grow, and I had the numbers to prove it. But at this meeting we were forced into voting on a course of action that I firmly believed would eventually lead to the closure of our newly planted congregation. My attempts to get in an outside expert to help us think in an informed way about multi-con-gregational models of church and what are now called 'Fresh

Expressions' were blocked: we had to vote *now*, and we had to vote in *this* way, or many more people, who were poised on the brink, would leave the church. In the event I was the only one on the PCC to vote against the proposal.

I went home that night broken: the next morning I just couldn't get out of bed. Later that day I went to my GP, who signed me off, for the first time in thirty-two years of ministry, with 'work-related stress'. That same day I went to visit a mental-health professional who was also a church vulnerable-adults protection officer, and I asked him what exactly constituted 'workplace bullying'. His answer was that, in the eyes of the law, someone has been bullied if they felt themselves to have been bullied, with a resulting detrimental effect on their health.[19] I qualified on both counts!

I had a couple of weeks off work, followed immediately by a holiday which we had already booked, and I had time to lick my wounds and decide where to go from there. As you can imagine there was much heart-searching. I had always thought of myself as thick-skinned and broad-shouldered: I had always had a strong sense of determination and an ability to handle conflict relatively unscathed, but all that seemed to have deserted me as I faced hostility from the people I was supposed to be loving and leading. I realised I had become paranoid too: whenever I saw people talking in groups after services I was convinced they were talking about me, a feeling which remains uncomfortable to me to this day. But along with the realisation of the depth of my failure came a new determination to stick to my guns and find a way to win through. After a family prayer-time, we resolved not to give in.

When I did finally make it back to work the pressure only intensified, and peaked again at a series of meetings, presided over by a hierarch from the diocese, at which my faults, failings and behaviour were discussed in my presence. Things were also becoming increasingly painful for my family: Chris, who headed up the new service, became a target for persecution, which was even more painful for me than my own troubles. In the end, my new determination notwithstanding, I threw in the towel. I went to see the bishop and told him that for the sake of my health and that of my family I had to get out. I had tried to recover my sense of call and purpose, but in the face of such hostility I just couldn't take it anymore. It was with a sense of abject failure and heart-freeing relief that I emerged from the bishop's office that day.

Meanwhile though, from another direction, things were happening. For most of my ministry I have had in my mind two dreams. One was to teach in a theological college, and the other was to study for a doctorate. Back in 1996 I had my one and only sabbatical from ministry, which, apart from travelling to Canada and the USA, I used to write a research thesis on Music and Emotion (that's another story). I was being supervised by someone who worked at a Cambridge college, and I can remember one visit very clearly. It was a beautiful day in late May or early June; the spring sun was shining, and one whole wall of the quad was covered in wisteria (one of my very favourite flowers) in glorious bloom. I can remember sitting in the chapel before morning prayer, and saying to God with all the earnest longing of my heart 'Please, please, please let me come and work in a place like this!' When I accepted the job at St Basil's, which I knew was to be my final job before retirement, I knew that I had kissed goodbye to the first of my dreams. What I came to think of as my wisteria prayer had not been answered, or at least not positively. However, I still might be able to fulfil the second. I have a friend who, at the time, was course director for a London-based Doctor of Ministry course, and so I spent a day at King's, my old college, enquiring about the possibility of my doing the doctorate as part of my in-service training. It was all fine: I could easily get onto the course, it would only demand a day or two per week of study and the course fees would be £1,800 per year for the next six years, plus regular travel to London. That put paid to that idea too: there was no way I could make that kind of financial commitment, even if I could get some grant help towards it.

Just before Christmas I had seen an advert in the *Church Times* for someone to teach liturgy (my specialist subject) at an Anglican theological college. I held out little hope: I had applied for such posts many times over the years, and the answer was always the same: if you wanted to teach you had to have a PhD. But as things were not going smoothly at St Basil's I decided there was nothing to lose in sending off for the details. They arrived, but at exactly the time I was return- ing from my sick leave with fresh determination to stay and make a go of it. I deleted the e-mail without even opening it, lest I be tempted from my chosen course of action. The closing date came and went, and I thought no more about it.

A couple of months later, two days before the final meeting with the PCC, I was away on a residential meeting with a bunch of fellow liturgists, where we discussed the publishing schedule for Grove Books and generally caught up with the latest liturgical gossip (yes, I agree, we probably do need to get out more). The latest piece of goss was that a well-known theological college had interviewed for a new liturgy tutor just before Christmas, but had failed to appoint and were now going to head-hunt. It was literally days after this that I took the decision to leave St Basil's, and shortly after that a good friend 'happened' to sit next to the college principal at a meeting. Did he know anyone who might be interested in the post? Well, as it happened he did. He mentioned my name. Apparently the principal had already thought of me and had looked me up, but seeing that I'd only been in my parish for a few years had discounted me as not being ready for a move yet.

So it was that a few days later I was in a garden centre when my mobile rang and a forty-five minute conversation ensued. This led to a visit to the college (which I knew well, having lectured and preached there on several occasions), and a subsequent interview. I was offered the job just before Easter, on one condition: I would have to do my doctorate, for which, since I would be working in the world of education, there would be all sorts of grants available. Interestingly as part of the interview I was shown around the house that goes with the job on the college campus. I couldn't help but notice that the front of it was covered with some brown twiggy plant or other, but I didn't think much of it. When I went back a couple of months later to measure it up, however, the whole of my front wall was gloriously ablaze with lilac flowers. It had taken him seventeen years, but finally God had answered my wisteria prayer.

In the meantime the diocese were very good to me and took me out of the parish and found some work for me in the diocesan office. I announced my departure from St Basil's at the very end of the service on Easter Sunday. I pulled no punches, telling the congregation that it had been decided almost a year ago that I should leave, and that I had felt disliked and bullied to the point where, for the sake of my health and that of my family, I had decided to resign. Whatever the rights and wrongs we had no option but to give up the fight and, in line with the wishes of 80 per cent of them, retire hurt. I then processed out and waited in the porch to see the reaction. I had always suspected that the 80 per cent might have been a bit of an exaggeration, but I was shocked to see tears, and to hear comments like 'We had no idea this was going on', 'We're so sorry you've been treated like this', 'We're ashamed to belong to a church that does this to people' and, overwhelmingly, 'Where did they get 80 per cent from? No-one ever asked me!' I discovered, or rather I got back in touch with the fact, that actually many people in the church loved me and valued my ministry. But because of a natural reluctance in the church to wash our dirty linen in public, most of the opposition to our ministry had taken place in the dark, behind closed doors. The first many people knew of any trouble at all was my resignation sermon, which left them with a deep sense of shock.

My final sermon, on Pentecost Sunday, consisted of an apology for all that I had done to contribute to this pastoral breakdown, and a call for a full, honest and public exploration into what had gone wrong. If things had been said in the name of the congregation, they had a right to know what and why. If this is all swept under the carpet, I told them, it *will* happen again. I also made the point that we had to distinguish between God's perfect will and his redemptive will. Sometimes things happen because that is always how God intended them to happen, but sometimes they happen because he is bringing good out of evil, working all things together for good for those who love him. I could not believe that this was the perfect will of God, but I was convinced that he could redeem, for me and for the church, if we let him.

I managed to survive the final bun fight with dignity, a couple of people found some genuinely positive and heart-felt things to say about me, reflecting the views of the silent majority, and those who had wanted for so long to end my ministry had the grace to keep a low profile. Then I made my excuses and left, and a huge weight fell from my shoulders.

While still living in the vicarage I was now free of the parish, free from the hostility of those who had opposed me, usefully although not gainfully employed in the dioce-san office, worshipping happily at the cathedral and looking forward to my dream job. But I had one more task to do, perhaps the most difficult of all: I had to forgive. It was a great insight when I heard someone define forgiveness as 'choosing to hand back to God the right to punish' those who have hurt us. I don't have to like them; I certainly don't have to trust them, but neither do I have to seek or plot my own revenge. Did Jesus' prayer for his torturers, 'Father, forgive them, for they do not know what they are doing' (Luke 23:34) mean 'Father, just let them off the hook' or 'Father, bring them to the point where they can see what they've done and are repentant so that you are able to forgive them'? We'll know one day, but what it clearly didn't mean was 'Father, smite them with all you've got.' But this insight was brought even more sharply into focus when I attended a three-line whip training day on child abuse. It was an extremely useful day, and pertinent to my situation.

Let me preface this section by saying that of course my sense of having been bullied and my experience of conflict in the church is nowhere on the spectrum of seriousness compared to the physical, emotional and sexual abuse of children, and I hope that you'll understand that I am not trying to compare the two. But two insights came out of the training day for me that showed me some interesting similarities which do bear reflecting on. Firstly, we were told that the rehabilitation of convicted sex offenders is virtually impossible. If you do have a convicted paedophile in your congregation, it is almost certain that he will try to reoffend. That is hard statistical fact, but it obviously raises some big questions about the grace of God and a theology of forgiveness. The fact is that those who sexually abuse children construct for themselves a fantasy world where such behaviour is perfectly acceptable, and they continue to live in that world. So what does it mean to forgive someone like that? A helpful theological paper by Stephen Tracy examined the nature of forgiveness in the Bible, and suggested that in most churches the received wisdom is woefully inadequate.[20] Many who have been abused in one way or another have been encouraged 'just to forgive and let go', but the biblical evidence is far more complex. In fact, Tracy suggests, there are three distinct understandings of forgiveness in the pages of Scripture.

The first is judicial forgiveness, the forgiveness of the perpetrator by God. This is between those two parties alone, and does not immediately affect us. We also know that for God to forgive requires repentance and contrition on the part of the sinner.

Secondly, there is what he calls 'psychological forgiveness'. This is the part I mentioned above: a refusal to seek personal revenge, and instead a handing over of the sinners into the hands of God, for him to forgive if he can and to punish if not. Once we have let go, the rest is up to him, but this element of forgiveness is not in any way dependent on repentance on the part of those we need to forgive. We just need to let them go, whether or not we feel they have expressed or felt regret.

And thirdly, there is 'relational forgiveness'. Can we be friends again with those who have so hurt us? Maybe, and maybe not, but it will certainly not happen unless we can see some signs of remorse, some understanding of the distress they have caused us and some resolve to behave differently in the future. So what this means is that for forgiveness to happen, two out of three elements require some recognition of sin and sorrow for it, and some understanding of the hurt it has caused.

Let me say again that I am not in any way wanting to compare in seriousness what I went through and what abused children suffer. But I do understand that my accusers genuinely believed that what they were doing was for the good of the church. They did not show the slightest signs of remorse or express any forgiveness towards me when I admitted faults and mistakes. In that sense I believe they constructed a fantasy world where the end justified the means because it was for the good of St Basil's (in their view). I find the prospect of restored relationships impossible at this time, because I do not see signs that they are sorry for what they have done. Whether or not God forgives them is between them and him, and is no business of mine. So the only thing I can do, and the only thing that is independent of any repentance or not on their part, is to let go of any desire for revenge and hand them into the loving but righteous care of God.

The same is true, to a lesser extent, of others in the church who were less active in their persecution but in a way just as hurtful. As Chris remarked, although a small number of people threw the stones, many more held their coats. People who would have called us friends sat through meetings where we were vilified without defending us. Again, in the culture of a church where conflict isn't addressed, this must have been very difficult for them, but to us it felt like betrayal. I identified strongly with the words of Martin Luther King, Jr.: 'In the end, we will remember not the words of our enemies, but the silence of our friends.' They too need our forgiveness, and God's, but restoration seems difficult, particularly as it seems they have no understanding of how deeply they have hurt and betrayed us. So sometimes it is within the mercies of God that we can simply go our separate ways. When we meet up in heaven we'll no doubt have a different perspective on things, but for now it seems like a gift of God that we can move north, shake the dust off our feet and begin again in my dream job.

So what did it feel like to have failed? It was certainly a new experience for me, at least to have failed in such a huge way.

It wasn't helped by well-meaning friends who tried to tell me that I hadn't really failed at all, and that I shouldn't feel bad about it. I was reminded of a conference at which John Wimber, whom we met in a previous chapter, was asked about the death of his good friend David Watson from cancer, in spite of hours of prayer and ministry. 'I wouldn't want you to feel you'd failed' said the questioner. John snapped back 'Is failure offensive to you? I fail several times each day'. I had set out to grow the best church in the diocese, and here I was: driven out, with the church a shadow of its former self. If that isn't failure, I don't know what is. And yet somehow that was OK.

Through it all I knew that I was OK with God. Not in the sense that I hadn't done anything wrong and it was all 'their' fault, but rather that even though I knew I had done plenty wrong I believed I had handled it correctly, with emotional intelligence and integrity. No-one may have expressed forgiveness to me for my mistakes, but I knew myself to be forgiven by God and right with him. The bishop had said to me that throughout this sad chapter I had acted with integrity. I knew myself to be a beloved child of God, a God who was deeply concerned about my pain and not in any way holding any of it against me. It's easy to know God's favour when things are going well, but somewhere along the way I had received an upgrade which allowed me to be assured of his favour even in the middle of mess and failure. I'm very disappointed, of course, at the way things worked out, but I can honestly say I don't feel that the experience has dented my relationship with my loving Father. And I've learnt over again that there is nothing offensive about failure if we handle it well.

One of the questions I was asked in my interview for the college job was, 'What have you learnt from the experience of St Basil's?' Apart from the above about forgiveness, and a determination never to tell someone that they've 'just got to forgive' someone who has devastated them, three things stood out, all of which I'm proud of but in very different ways.

First of all, I believe God has upgraded my sense of my own vulnerability. Feeling bullied was something that happened to other people, not me. I've fought and won may battles over the years, and I'm the boss. But I had to be taken down a peg or two, and God reminded me with this download that I'm as vulnerable and susceptible to hard knocks as anyone else. That has been an incredibly useful lesson to learn, and I am glad to be on the way to learning it.

Secondly, I have realised that you can't simply take past successes and repeat them in new settings. I don't think my ministry in Dorset was fundamentally different from anywhere else. It's just that the soil wasn't conducive, and/or that my approach was inappropriate. That too is a humbling lesson to learn, and I wish I'd had that particular download a lot earlier in my life.

But thirdly, I have learnt a great deal about my professionalism. The fact is that with all this turmoil going on I still managed to conduct services, visit ill people, take weddings and funerals – and even to pray. Being a priest, as with many jobs, requires a certain amount of 'acting' the role even when you don't feel like it: I would be of no help at all to grieving families if I were to break down myself during the funeral service, or to spend all my time during a hospital visit moaning about my own woes. I define professionalism as knowing the right time and place to be yourself and when not to. In a different way I feel pleased that through the grace of God I have managed to maintain enough inner strength to function in my role, at least for the vast majority of the time.

My vulnerability, however, was to appear as never before as I prepared for my new role.

14

The Final Chapter?

I asked in the last chapter what could possibly go wrong. I was out of trouble, headed for my dream job, the wisteria was in bloom and everything else in the garden was in a right mess because we were leaving so there was no point in weeding.

Then yesterday I was diagnosed with cancer. In fact it began with a toothache about three months ago. In the end my dentist gave me an urgent referral to hospital, where after a biopsy the consultant confirmed that it was mouth cancer, and that I would need surgery and radiotherapy.

I guess I'm writing this in a bit of shock, although to be honest my predominant feeling is relief because I've suspected for several weeks that that was what was going on. But in the light of working on this book I have been fascinated to observe myself coping with what is one of the greatest dreads people have. 'What I feared has come upon me; what I dreaded has happened to me' said the tormented Job (Job 3:25), and who does not fear the 'C' word? Who indeed has not in some dark moments imagined how they might cope with a diagnosis like this? I realised that I have the opportunity, and something of a ringside seat, to answer that question for myself. So as I attempt to stand at a bit of a distance from myself and observe my reactions, what do I see?

Before I say anything about that, though, I do need to make a disclaimer. I can only write about what I can see now. Many people have travelled the road that lies ahead of me, and they will have far more idea than I have of the ups and downs to come. So I reserve the right further on in the journey to disprove dramatically anything I'm writing now. I may well fall to pieces, or plunge into depression, or lose my faith or whatever. I just don't know. At the moment I don't feel at all ill. Apart from a pain and some swelling in the side of my mouth I'm perfectly able to continue life as normal, driving, writing books, you know the kind of thing. I can eat and drink pretty normally, except that I can't open my mouth very wide. So I have to live on thin things like crisps, slices of salami and pitta breads. But I suspect that the not-feeling-ill phase may not last! So you need to read this chapter as a snapshot of where I am today, hot on the heels of my diagnosis.

The first thing I notice is the total lack of any kind of 'Why me?' feelings. So often when bad things happen to us our immediate reaction is of a great sense of injustice, as though we somehow deserved immunity from life's knocks. Other people have told me already that it doesn't seem fair, and on one level that's true, but then life isn't fair. Nobody ever suggested it should be. Having walked with people through journeys like the one I now face during the course of my pastoral ministry, my (of course unspoken) answer to their 'Why me?' questions has always been 'Why *not* you?' The fact is that things happen, we get ill; sometimes we get very ill. I now regret smoking when I was younger, because that is somewhere in the mix of factors that cause some people to get cancer, but I can also remember a young man in one of my parishes who was a fit and healthy sportsman who had never had a cigarette in his life contracting lung cancer and dying within six weeks of the diagnosis, leaving a distraught widow and two young kids. It isn't fair: that's the point.

The next thing I observe is a surprising bravery and determination. I have watched quite a few people go on the cancer journey over the years, and I have always told my family that if anything like that happened to me I didn't want to go through months of therapy that feels even worse than the illness. I would refuse treatment, and do all I could to die as painlessly as possible. Better to get it over with than to be a burden to my family and make them watch a long, drawn-out decline. But I find that suddenly I've changed my mind, and I'm determined to get through this. Of course no-one is saying this is terminal, and at 60 I don't yet feel old enough to die, but I am surprised at where this determination has come from. Of course I reserve the right of anyone to feel that the road ahead is just too hard for them, but that isn't how I feel, and I find myself amazed by that fact.

I am reminded, though, that actually I learnt this lesson many years ago. Our elder son Steve, when he was 4, became ill and was diagnosed with meningitis. It was every parent's nightmare, but again I discovered that when the chips are really down you somehow find the resources from somewhere just to get on with it, do what needs doing and get through it. I can remember a friend telling us not to worry about praying, because we probably wouldn't be able to, but that we had plenty of other people doing it for us. That's one reading of James 5: 13–14, which, I'd heard once in a sermon, was all about keeping in touch with God. 'In a mess? Then pray. Happy? Then praise. Ill? Then call the elders and get them to do your praying for you' (paraphrase). I don't actually believe that is what James meant, as the next verse makes clear, but there is truth there, and we literally felt buoyed up on the prayers of others, even though we were too distraught inside to make much sense with our own prayers. I feel a bit like that now. And when, after ten days in an isolation hospital out on the moors near Sheffield, Steve began to rally, we knew that those prayers had been answered. The way we were told, by some junior doctor who breezed in cheerily at 4:30 a.m. and said, 'It looks like we're going to keep him!' may have left something to be desired, but we learnt an important lesson from that: most of the time, you cope. The human spirit, and particularly the human spirit buoyed up on faith and prayer, is an amazingly resilient thing. God has built into us, whether we acknowledge him or not, the ability to cope with a lot more than we think we can.

I do seem also to have managed to retain some sense of perspective and humour about the whole thing. There are many times in my life when I have tried to be depressed. I have thought that the prospect of three months off and some strong medication looked very attractive, but that feeling has never lasted more than a day or two. I wouldn't have said that I'm that much of an optimist, but I've found on several occasions that I seem unable to sustain the feelings of being totally down and out for very long at a time. I have always found myself, often much to my annoyance, managing to crack a joke and see the funny side of everything.

Although at this stage no-one seems to be saying that my cancer is terminal, I do think a lot about death. I can remember reaching the stage in the past when, without actually praying it, I could understand those in the Bible who had said to God, 'I've had enough: just let me die now.' As I've got older heaven has become far more real to me, and far more of a living hope than somewhere I'm not interested in yet, thank you very much.

When I worked in Wales my boss, Bishop Dominic of Monmouth, had to go into hospital for a quadruple bypass operation, an operation that was not only going to be done under local anaesthetic, but was also going to be broadcast on television. Dominic insisted that he had allowed permission for his operation to be shown so that the clergy of his diocese could see beyond any doubt that he did actually have a heart, and we certainly saw bits of him we'd never seen before. But the one thing that stands out for me from the programme was the interview before the operation, bizarrely conducted for reasons that I shall never fully understand by celebrity chef Ainsley Harriott, during which Dominic was asked if he was afraid of death. He replied brightly, 'There are a lot worse things that can happen to Christians than death.' I shall never forget those words, or the confidence that Dominic showed in his deep faith in a deeply faithful God.

I am, of course, frightened by the thought of the process of dying, mainly because I'm allergic to pain, and a man to boot. But after many years of visits to dentists I've learnt that pain lasts for a relatively short time, and that the feeling when you come out and it's all over for another six months is like walking on air. All you have to do is grit your teeth and go through it, because soon it will all stop. (Actually on reflection gritting your teeth at the dentist's isn't a great idea, but you know what I mean.) There's a picture of heaven for you, and I hope that if I do eventually go through some sort of agonising final throes those words won't come back to haunt me.

I've read through this chapter so far and I realise that I'm coming over as some kind of super-saint, bravely facing trials and tribulations with unwavering faith in God, a doubt-free hope of heaven and a stubborn refusal to get miserable about it all. I think I'm as surprised at this as anyone, and if you think I'm a superhero you should see me during the sleepless nights when the spectres of 'What if?' come out to haunt me. I can simply report that this is how it is for me: I'm not 'trying' to be brave, or working up some superhuman levels of faith. It's just what I'm doing, and I wonder if actually most of us would not find the same degree of surprise were we faced with the same thing. Indeed many people have found it, and have dealt victoriously with serious illness, whether or not it got them in the end.

The acid test of any faith or philosophy is, of course, how it helps us cope through hard times. It's all very well for someone to claim to believe in reincarnation or something: the question is how that belief actually helps when life kicks you in the teeth. All kinds of people believe in all kinds of things: that's why it is inaccurate for Christians to say that we're 'saved by faith'. Faith is merely the tow-rope to rescue us and get us out of trouble. What really matters is what we tie the tow rope onto. If we choose an AA van, that's likely to be a safe bet, but a No. 52 bus might get us into all kinds of trouble. Faith is what ties us onto Jesus, and his saving work on the cross, but faith can also be severely misplaced. But all in all I do feel pleased that so far my faith (and quite a bit of ibuprofen) do seem to be sustaining me, and giving me courage and that kind of peace that passes understanding because there's absolutely no way I should feel peaceful right now. I certainly haven't found myself railing at God, or wanting to take my spiritual ball away and go home just because things haven't gone nicely for me.

I'm also aware, although I don't really buy all the self-help 'make friends with your tumour' kind of stuff, that stress can be a factor both in getting cancer in the first place and in getting over it.[21] I guess my life has been about as stressful as your average person's, and possibly quite a bit more so recently. I'll never know if there has been any kind of causal link between the persecution I've suffered over the past four years and my cancer. It would be easy and tempting to think that 'It's all their fault!' but I just can't say with any certainty if that is true, or even if just a little bit of it might be their fault. I've got it, so that's that. Let's get to hospital as soon as I can, and get rid of it as effectively as the doctors can.

But when it comes to recovery I do think I have something in my favour. I've never been a workaholic. The C of E has seen to that: they don't pay me enough to demand my life 24/7. If I were on a six figure salary I might consider not bothering with days off or coming back early from holidays because someone needs me at a meeting, but not on what they pay me. Neither do I suffer from what I call 'Saviour of the Universe Syndrome', where if I don't do something there's absolutely no-one else who can do it. In fact there are plenty of people who can do it, if they've a will to, although of course they'll do it differently from the way I might do it. Or they won't, and it won't get done. That's not my fault. So the prospect of six months of my life being spent with no 'shoulds' or 'oughts' but simply time to chill and recover doesn't fill me with anxiety. The reality may of course prove to be very different, but at this stage I have no intention of feeling guilty about being ill. I will try to be considerate to my family and those who will be looking after me, and I hope eventually I'll get bored and want to do something useful, but I'm certainly not going to try to find things to feel guilty about, or things I should have done to worry about. I hope I can relax into 'being ill' mode and as far as possible enjoy the freedom of it.

Obviously the question of healing is on my mind. I think I'm with Shadrach, Meshach and Abednego (Dan. 3). The God whom I serve is able to heal me miraculously, I have no doubt of that, but even if he does not, I have no intention of worshipping anyone else instead. I believe in healings, and as I've said I've seen a few, but if I'm honest not as many as I would have liked, so I can't in all honesty say I'm in some great place of powerful faith and 'believing for a miracle'. I certainly don't feel that I deserve one, in preference to the many people who die even in spite of prayer. Another friend's gift to me in the past was the insight that there is often a huge gap between 'the real' and 'the true'. There are things that I believe are true, and I would stake my life on them, but in my experience they're not always real, and don't always work out. Living in the gap between the true and the real is a difficult thing to do, but we all have to find a way to do it somehow. So I am not closed or faithless to the idea of miraculous healing, but I rather suspect I might have to go through the journey of medical care instead.

I can remember many years ago reading *The Power to Heal* by Francis MacNutt, an early pioneer of the healing ministry, where he says:

> I must get out of the habit of thinking of all people . . . as healed by prayer or not healed by prayer. I should rejoice if many – or even some – of the people I pray for . . . are improved in health. I want to grow closer in union with Jesus Christ so that more of his life, his wisdom, his authority and his healing power will work through me to heal others.[22]

He talks about both complete healing but also degrees of healing: lessened pain, freedom from side effects of drugs and so on. I believe that I have already seen some physical changes in myself as a result of prayer ministry, but I know I am far from cured. So I'm happy for anyone and everyone to pray for me, but I don't feel at this stage as though I'm likely to throw a tantrum and walk away from God if the miracle doesn't happen.

I must also put on record the care with which the medical professionals have treated me so far. I know it's easy to moan about the NHS, and I'm sure as an institution it does have some systemic issues, but the individuals who have cared for me so far have been nothing but kind, gentle and sympathetic. I especially liked the nurse who told me that my particular consultant was one of the top head and neck surgeons in the whole of the south of England, and that I was in the best possible hands, although I couldn't help but note that never, either in real life or on the telly, have I heard anyone being told, 'Your consultant's not bad. He's the best we could get in the price range, but he'll probably do a reasonable job on you, fingers crossed!' I'm also very aware of the privilege of living in a country where we do have an NHS, and that financial hardship is not going to be added to the trauma of my treatment.

How will it all end? I have no idea, only some hopes and some good intentions. I understand that St Paul said that 'hope does not disappoint us' (Rom. 5:5, NRSV) but I also know how often it does. I believe that Paul was talking about the ultimate reality of the Kingdom of God, and that after the trials and pain of this life there will be a glorious future awaiting us, even though in the meantime life may well get as disappointing as it is possible to be.

I'm also aware that it may feel as though this book is deliberately left hanging, like those films where you just know that they've left room for a money-spinning sequel, which will not be anywhere near as good as the original, but people won't discover that until they've paid to see it. So if you're thinking that I'm keeping the door open for *God's Upgrades II – Revenge of the Radiotherapists* you might be right. You'll need to have a word with my publishers about that.

Epilogue

I t's now three months later, and by the fact that this bit isn't headed 'Epilogue by Chris Leach' you'll have gathered that I survived. My editor thought you might like an update rather than a sequel, and in line with the theme of this book I thought I should share a few reflections and experiences on my journey since my cancer diagnosis.

I was admitted pretty quickly into the fictitious Royal Dorset hospital, and underwent eighteen hours of surgery, which involved taking away all the cancerous tissue and bone from my jaw, rebuilding it with the help of a metal plate, a piece of bone about the size of a Mars bar from the front of my pelvis and a large lump of muscle from my hip, which was reconnected to some blood vessels in my face. Then I spent forty-eight hours in intensive care, a further eight days in a normal ward and then went home to recuperate, missing the return to the bosom of my family in time for our joint birthdays by just one day.[23] I must record my thanks to the good people of Costa Coffee in the hospital lobby who graciously allowed us to have a birthday party in their shop, even providing plates and a large knife for the cake that Chris brought in. Steve, Vicki, Paul and his new bride Jenni were there, and it is a birthday Chris and I won't forget in a hurry. I was then passed on to the oncologist to arrange six weeks of daily radiotherapy, and six sessions of chemo.

I'm sure that some people reading this will already have been through a similar process, but that for the majority the prospect of having to do so is one of their greatest dreads, as it had always been one of mine. Everyone's journey is unique, of course, and I can only speak of mine, which so far has had a positive outcome, but I think that what I want to say above all is that actually it hasn't been too bad.

First of all, it most certainly has not been a painful journey. This was a huge surprise to me. Think of cancer, or indeed major surgery, and one's first reaction is often the fear of extreme physical pain. For me that was simply not the case, apart from one small unfortunate incident that was down to human error and which, with hindsight, was quite amusing. It has been uncomfortable at times, but never more than that. And where there was some pain, in the first forty-eight hours after surgery, it was in my hip from where they had removed some bone and muscle, rather than in my face where they had stuck it back again, and then only when I tried to move. If I just lay still I couldn't feel a thing. Even from there, within a week I went for a quarter of a mile walk and climbed up and down two staircases with comparative ease. One would expect after eighteen hours of surgery some fairly major cocktails of knock-out drugs, but for most of the time I was in hospital I had nothing but paracetamol. By the eighth day after surgery I didn't even bother with that. Every time anyone came in to do anything to me, the first question was 'Are you in pain?' It seemed that even the ladies who emptied the bins asked me (although I guess they may have needed a higher authority actually to prescribe anything). There was always more analgesia available, but I never asked for any, and I'm a real coward. So if you live with some great unexpressed fears about absolute agony, you really don't need to. And apparently this is equally true for cases far more tragic than mine: the whole hospice movement is based on the ability of the medical profession nowadays to manage pain with a high degree of effectiveness. The people whom this hurts, I was told before my operation, are the people too proud or too daft to let on that they're hurting.

Sickness is, I think, another fantasy that haunts many people. I'm not a 'sicky' person generally, but there were two occasions, one in response to some of my 'food' and one to a particular drug, when I began to feel a bit nauseous, a feeling that like most people I find very unpleasant, but also quite scary when you're not supposed to make any violent movements to your face. The nurse could obviously see me go pale, and so on both occasions I was immediately given an injection that *instantly* stopped the sick feeling. And talking of injections, yes, they did pump quite a bit of stuff into me, in the early days particularly, but I wasn't a pincushion: they put in a cannula, which is a kind of needle with a stopcock into your vein. Once it's in all injections can go in via that route, so if you 'hate needles' you really only do need one, which goes in just before they knock you out for the operation.

Discomfort is another matter, though. For at least a fortnight I was unable to get more than two hours sleep each night, due to the need to balance several factors. Obviously in the very early days they wanted to keep my head as still as possible. But when you keep still you have three dangers: pressure sores on the bits of your body you're lying on, chest infections due to fluid getting stuck on your lungs and blood clots (or 'deep vein thromboses') usually in your legs. The answer to all the above is to put silly socks on and keep moving, but to do that while keeping still: not an easy task.[24] So in the intensive care unit (ITU) they had these special beds that do your moving for you, but only the bits that they want to move. Very effective in my case, but not a great aid to a good night's kip. The feeling of complete exhaustion without being able actually to sleep isn't painful, but it is pretty uncomfortable and draining.

Speech is another balancing act in the case of an operation like mine. Muscles very quickly waste away if not used, so normally they would want you to talk as much as possible as soon as possible. But in my case they wanted to keep my mouth as still as possible for as long as possible, so again I had to be careful. In fact they were very impressed by my speech but, as I told them, I do it for a living so it'd take a lot more than a neck dissection to stop me.

Because of the nature of my particular surgery, I had to be nil-by-mouth for around two weeks. While I was knocked out for surgery they put a tube up one nostril and down into my stomach, through which I was fed with various colours of nutritious jollop via a pump. Later on I had four hours reprieve per day during which I was disconnected from the machine and could go walkabout around the hospital. Again this wasn't painful, but it was a real nuisance. I could talk, but I sounded really strange. I remember the day, about a week after surgery, when I was allowed half a thimbleful of mouthwash four times a day. Forget the single malts: this was the most beautiful taste in the world. A few days later a consultant came and taught me how to take a sip of water. I practised all evening, and the next morning, when I obviously hadn't drowned or had it come out of my ears, and still had the ability to swallow, I was brought a large mug of coffee, my first for nine days. I can remember texting my son, after one particularly good night: 'Just woken from two hours kip and had mint mouthwash. Such simple pleasures change one's perspective on life.'

The other big issue for me was the physical look of my face. It's a complicated procedure but the muscle from my hip that had been used for walking around was going to be used now for things like eating and smiling, which would require a lot less hard work of it, even with the amount I eat (and smile). So in order that it would atrophy, or waste away, eventually to the point where my face was symmetrical, they had, as Paul described it, to 'staple half a football to the side of my face'. After three months the swelling would reduce and my head would once more look normal. I asked Chris to do two things for me: to take a photo of my head as soon as possible after surgery, but not show it to me for three months, and to put cards over all the mirrors in my room when I went from ITU to the ward. I just did not want to see what I looked like, and I guessed that the people who came from time to time to suck some blood out of me might feel more comfortable with the mirrors covered up too.

The first time my family saw me they said they were really surprised at how awful I *didn't* look, but they would say that, wouldn't they? I think they had expected some kind of mummy horror-film look with my entire upper body swathed in blood-oozing bandages and just my eyes peeping out: in fact my face had no dressings at all on it, just a neat row of staples running along a crease under my chin and hidden by stubble. But I still didn't want to know. So the covering-up-the-mirrors ploy worked well until a few days in when I felt well enough to boot up my laptop and begin my journey through my *Spooks* box sets. There's a phase of the boot sequence built in deliberately by Microsoft for vain post-operatives when for a few seconds the screen becomes an almost perfect mirror and I caught the full horror of my new look out of the blue. That, I have to say, *was* traumatic, and the fact that in three months' time I'd look normal did nothing but focus me on the fact that for three months I would look decidedly abnormal. Even in my wanderings round the hospital I could see people looking pityingly at me. I could just foresee the time in some public place when a young child would say in a loud stage whisper, 'Mummy, why has that man got half a football stapled onto his face?' I knew I'd got some work to do here, but praise the Lord for hoodies. I have to say that my friends and family have been enormously encouraging about this, and not even once has anyone used the term 'Elephant Man' in my hearing. If there's one thing worse than having it all go pear-shaped, it's having half of it go pear-shaped. In fact by three weeks after surgery you'd have had to look pretty hard to see any swelling on my face: it was certainly less than before the operation.

Radiotherapy was interesting. Everyone had told me that I wouldn't feel anything for the first two or three weeks, but that it might get a bit uncomfortable after that. But I subsequently discovered that reactions are as individual as the people who have them, and that for some it hits like a sledgehammer from day one, but then you get used to it and it's not too bad. I discovered that I am of the second persuasion: the first week was really uncomfortable, and for one day quite painful, but after that I got used to it. One day early on I was tempted by an ASDA Scorchingly Hot Chicken Vindaloo. 'Can you handle the heat?' asked the label, thus ensuring that any bloke who saw it would buy it instantly. Now that *was* painful, and I'm sure it killed far more cells off than any radiotherapy, but my dietician was really impressed with me (although she did also say that she thought I was barking mad too).

I think that's enough medical stuff (note to self: get a proper doctor to read this bit, especially the bit about socks) but let me come back to where I started, and simply say that in comparison to my fantasies the whole experience has been nowhere near as dreadful, scary or traumatic. I know that some of you will be thinking, 'Good for you: you were always going to get better!' But what I think God has downloaded into me through all this is the confidence that even if I do one day face a terminal diagnosis, that might not be as bad as I would have expected either. It comes back to my son Steve and his meningitis again: God has put into the human spirit the ability to cope with a lot more than we think we can cope with. I might not have died through this experience of cancer, but a lot of my fear has, and that is why I thought this final section might be important for others too.

In fact, in line with the thesis of this whole book, I discovered that this phase has been incredibly spiritually enriching, in many different ways. I have found myself enormously grateful to God for so many things. I know that I'm getting close to the danger of writing some sickly sentimental Christian drivel at this point, but I hope you feel you know me well enough by now to know that I don't do drivel if I can help it. But in so many ways I'm grateful for what has obviously been God's hand on my life. I mentioned, for example, right at the start of this book, losing five and a half stone because a friend recommended a diet to me. While at the time that seemed a really good thing to have done, I now realise that it was more than that. I can imagine going through the last four months weighing 18 stone rather than 13: it may well have had a very different outcome. One day a nurse came and filled in some health and safety form with me, which contained the following questions: Could I get around unaided at home? Had I had a fall in the last year? Could I manage stairs unaided? Did I ever fall out of bed? I told her I regularly walked seven miles, I went to the gym three times a week and could run five kilometres. I'd just had a toothache, that was all. So even back two years ago I could see God's hand preparing me for this. (By the way, it is neither a theological nor a medical truth that if you've been on a diet recently it's because you're going to get cancer next year.)

Another spiritual uplift came less than a week after I came home from hospital. A couple of weeks before my surgery, when I still didn't know when I would be going in, the phone rang. It was my son Steve, in a highly excited mood. He had just moved from Bournemouth to Winchester, and had picked up a flyer about the forthcoming Winchester Festival of the Arts. The opening concert, which was to be held in early July in the cathedral featured – guess what – Berlioz's *Te Deum*. Did I want tickets? Would I be well enough to travel?

Would I even be out of hospital? There was much agonising, but two things clinched it for me. First, I looked on the festival's website and discovered that Berlioz was just the warm-up act for the major piece of the concert: Saint-Saëns' *Organ Symphony*. Unbeknown to Steve this was another of my favourite works: to hear that and the Berlioz together was bliss indeed. But the real clincher came when Chris asked me which would make me most upset: to buy the tickets and be stuck in hospital, or to be out of hospital and well enough but unable to go because we hadn't bought tickets? So by faith I booked a couple of seats, and in the mercy of God we were able to go. The concert was, as expected, magnificent, although I think it was marginally better in Coventry when I was singing. A couple of days away in Winchester did us both the world of good too. I even managed to drive some of the way.

I thank God, obviously, for the human skills of the medical profession and the associated technology that means that so many illnesses do not nowadays automatically bring with them the inevitable sentence of an agonising death. Obviously before my operation my focus was on the surgeons, and the amazing things that are now possible. But the experience of ITU and beyond showed me the other side. As one friend put it, the surgeons are merely the plumbers: the work of keeping the systems flowing after some fairly major rearrangement is every bit as skilled and exacting. Then there is the whole army of associated trades: pathologists to identify the types of cancer, oncologists to decide the most appropriate treatment plan, speech therapists to make you eat yoghurt while they have their hands round your throat – an interesting experience that I confess I had not had before – dieticians, physiotherapists, you name it, and every single one of them not just skilled in their secret arts but also gentle, loving and sympathetic in the extreme to their nervous and often bewildered patients.

I thank God as well for Facebook and associated technology. One of the most surprising things in this whole journey is the phenomenal number of people from just about every period of our lives who have found out and made contact. OK, I have had a wide and varied ministry, but when we tried to tot up the number of churches and individuals who have said that they are praying for us we made literally thousands. The first time I cried through this whole business wasn't when I was initially diagnosed: it was when Steve said he'd had a Facebook message from his friend Cynthia from his school in Coventry, whom he hadn't seen for fifteen years or so, wishing me well. People often say that you can help fight cancer by keeping a positive mental attitude, and to be honest I've always found that idea complete bunkum and self-help candy, but I would never have believed what a boost it has given me to know that so many people are praying (or at least rooting) for me. 'That's because they love you!' said Chris. Actually, I have discovered, being loved, and being told that you're loved, can be immensely important, especially when you've lived through the last year being told that 80 per cent of people can't stand you. I realise that there is a law of diminishing returns at work here, but in the early days when I needed it most I would not have believed the difference it made to me. So our daily Facebook updates and their resultant likes or replies have been far, far more significant than I ever would have thought possible. That in turn has made me ask myself how I might be a bit more sympathetic to the troubles of others.

Then of course there's the whole Christian witness bit, which has been a bit like IKEA but with less lifting and more injections. Chris made me a small display of family photos for my room, and because the most recent family event was Paul's wedding, there were a couple of me in my vicar's kit. As always, staff were surprised to know of my trade, but it brought out of the woodwork other Christians and, more significantly, seekers. Also, it was always my stated intent to be perceived by the staff as 'a good patient', and I really do believe that, as at IKEA, my evangelistic potential in the hospital has been powerful. So when one of the nurses let on that 'everyone likes you' and that 'you're really easy to look after' that felt like a boost too. My philosophy of people touching my life, often for short periods but leaving me something unforgettable, works the other way too, and my hope and prayer is that some of the people I have met on this particular journey will have been enriched by having known me.

I think God has also downloaded into me an even stronger awareness of vulnerability and dependence. Anyone who has ever had to go into hospital will have learnt very quickly that the first thing to let go of is your dignity. And yet there has never for one second been any sense that my dignity has been taken away from me. Nurses have ranged from nervous students to efficient, experienced professionals; from mumsy to matey, but to have been treated with such care so consistently has been an incredible experience of love. I remember two stars particularly: a beautiful young student nurse who used to come and clean gunk out of my eyes in the morning with such gentleness that I could really believe that she found it as much of a privilege as I did, and who then told me what beautiful long eyelashes I have. The other was a very new student, about 9 years old by the look of her, who happened to catch me on a bad day when I was a bit upset about the size of my face. I pointed to my photos, and I told her that was what I looked like when I was normal. She took the time to sit down with me and tell me I *was* normal, I was beautiful and soon I'd look beautiful again. I remain immensely grateful both to her and her guide dog for the compliment.

And of course I am thrilled about the sense of God's closeness throughout my treatment, both as I was well enough again to pick up my regular daily prayer, and also in those times when there was only one set of footprints and I could do nothing but let myself be carried. Among the paraphernalia I took into hospital to stop myself going stir-crazy was my MP3 player, which I usually take to the gym with me. In order to keep the element of surprise alive I always set it to 'shuffle', and I found it both amusing and tremendously comforting that when I could finally face listening to music again the first two tracks that popped up happened to be Bobby McFerrin's cheery, but if I'm honest somewhat superficial, advice 'Don't worry; be happy' followed by the piece I have chosen to be carried in to at my funeral.[25] Call it merely wishful thinking, but I'm sure a little voice in my head said to me, 'You won't be needing this for a few years yet!'

The greatest thanks must go to my family, who remain the dearest people to me, and without whom I would have found the whole thing so much more difficult. Steve took time off work to be with Chris over the surgery period: she was dreading leaving me at the hospital and driving home the night before, and seeing me for the first time afterwards. For both those occasions Steve was a tower of strength to her, and to me when he came to visit. Vicki, who was sitting her A levels during the time of my surgery was also struggling with a really bad cold, and so didn't want to come to hospital to infect me. It was lovely to see her a few days later, and probably good that she didn't see me at my worst. And Paul, who came with Jenni for the first weekend, continued his usual ministry of mocking me unmercifully, which was just what I needed at this stage as I was just about physically able to laugh again. Each day after the visit Chris and Vicki would go home and send out an e-mail update to all our friends, and put the latest on Facebook. This too was a real labour of love. I thank God that we've always been a close family and got on very well most of the time, but I came to value them more and more, the more vulnerable I was personally. Some of the most profound days were immediately after the surgery when I either couldn't talk or couldn't be bothered to, but we just sat holding hands.

Finally let me return to the question of healing, which I touched on earlier. There were some, I think, among the thousands of supporters, who had the faith to believe for a miracle, that the surgeon would have a look just before the operation only to discover that it had all gone away and I was healed. He and his team would then fall on their knees and acknowledge Jesus as Lord. Well, that didn't happen. But a lot more did. I lost five and a half stone in weight. My dentist was quick off the mark in getting me a referral. My pre-operative scans showed that the cancer had not spread but was very localised and completely operable. The surgeon told me the morning after the op that when he actually cut me open there were no surprises at all: he found exactly what the MRI scan had told him to expect: nothing more, nothing less. The operation went textbook: there were no complications, the arterial plumbing worked first time, the grafted muscle took perfectly. I got neither bed sores, chest infections nor DVT (although I did get socks, but I hope they may clear up soon). I wasn't sick. I recovered quickly, well and with no setbacks at all. My speech and mobility returned exceptionally quickly. I took to drinking and subsequently eating instantly and successfully (although to be fair neither of those have ever been a problem for me). One Christian nurse told me that every now and then you meet someone whom you just know is going to make a good recovery, and that she had seen that in me. On the morning of my discharge my consultant told me that my recovery had been 'stunning'. At a subsequent outpatients appointment another doctor told me my recovery was 'amazing' and 'couldn't be better'. The next time I met him he had the results from the analysis of the bits they'd taken out, and it turned out to be nowhere as bad as they'd thought. This meant that I didn't need to have chemotherapy after all. Staff liked me and found me great to work with. One nurse went to church with his mate for the first time as a result of our conversations. I feel a completely different person after the experience; much less fearful, much more caring, much, much more loved.

So was all that about answered prayer? And here comes the $64,000 question: if I could go back and choose either to go through the same again or experience a *bona fide* instant miracle instead, which would I choose? You know what? I find that question really hard to answer.

Postscript

I'm not sure if a postscript should come before or after an epilogue, or even if this book has far too many endings, but two major things have happened that you ought to know about if you've survived this far.

The good news is that now I'm almost at the end of my radiotherapy. The bad news, though, is that a few days ago I received a phone call from the college to which I had been appointed. Apparently a huge financial crisis had unexpectedly come to light recently. An emergency council meeting was called, at which it was decided that radical action had to be taken. The principal was despatched from the meeting to break the news to me and three other new members of staff that their jobs were no longer on offer. I had been officially appointed, but now I had to be dis-appointed. You can imagine what it felt like to have been not just offered but appointed to your dream job, only to have it snatched away from you. All sorts of questions, theological and practical, suddenly hit us.

I have to say that I don't blame the people at the college, at least not the current ones. I understand only too well what it is to come new into a post and only gradually discover the depth of the financial mess that has been left to you: I've done it several times in the course of my own ministry. I understand perfectly that sometimes you reach the point where painfully drastic action has to be taken, and taken *now*. I was told that this was about the hardest phone call he had ever had to make, and I can quite believe it. But suddenly, in the middle of a course of radiotherapy, I found myself jobless, potentially homeless and stuck in Dorset. We were devastated.

Once the shock had abated a little we had to begin to rebuild some kind of hope and security. As I write the college and the diocese are working on a package that will give us some financial security, at least in the short term, as well as somewhere for the family to live. Just as the therapy is depleting my energy levels I have to begin the tortuous process of job hunting, and as you can imagine we all have a dreadful feeling of déjà vu, as we face potential homelessness once again. We can't help but remember that while we are likely to have financial security for six months, last time it took two and a half years to find a job. And at that stage I wasn't in my sixties and recovering from cancer, with a failed ministry behind me.

I'd love to be able to hold on and tell you how this all resolved, how God provided, just in the nick of time, something *even* better than my dream job, at a stipend of £300,000 and with a free Bugatti Veyron company car. But contracts have been signed and deadlines agreed, leaving both you and us with immense and unanswered questions about how on earth this is going to work out, and indeed what on earth God is up to in it all. I just don't know. Maybe that sequel is needed after all.

It is in the nature of downloads and upgrades that it is only sometimes with hindsight that you can understand what God has been doing through it all. To be honest I am as baffled as anyone as to why this latest door has slammed, why my dreams have been shattered as the wisteria petals drop off into the mud. I simply don't have any convincing theological rationale for it all nor, on a bad day, any expectation that I ever will. Actually I think if anyone did try to give me a nice Christian answer I'd probably punch them on the nose. So at the end of this book (and I promise this will be the end, finally) my only conclusion is a profoundly theological one – stuff (or worse) happens.

Richard Rohr's book, which a friend gave me during my radiotherapy, and from which I have already quoted a couple of times, is subtitled 'A spirituality for the two halves of life'. His thesis is that the first half of our lives is all about building a strong 'nest' of certainty and structure from which we can live the second half, which is about insecurity, questioning rather than certainty, failure, doubt and ambiguity. A mature faith is a lot less certain about pretty much anything than an immature one. Reading it I was reminded of another book, which was all the rage when I was a new curate, called *The Stature of Waiting*.[26] Vanstone's thesis is that Jesus' ministry was exercised in two halves. In the beginning he was in control: he decided, acted, travelled, preached, healed, questioned . . . But at his arrest there was a profound change. Jesus no longer *did*: he was *done to*. He moved from active to passive mode, as he was shunted from pillar to post, he was the one being questioned and, of course, finally he was tortured and murdered. Jesus' disciples were unable to understand why, even from the cross, Jesus wouldn't just *do* something to get himself out of the mess he was in, but Jesus seemed to accept the role of one being done to, and therefore gave dignity and stature to those of us who are the victims of life rather than its movers and shakers. Sometimes it is when we are most out of control, the most 'done to', that we are the most Christ-like.

As a young Christian I had spent hours agonising over things and their significance: why had God allowed this, that, or the other to happen, what was the deep meaning of this circumstance, what was God trying to say to me through that thing? While my breakdown was about letting go of some of this rather neurotic approach to life, I came to realise that it was still alive and well in me. Sometimes things just . . . happen. There is no great significance, or deep spiritual reason behind them. God isn't actually controlling each day-to-day event with all his minute attention to detail. We're not pieces on a huge chessboard being moved around by a deity who is either mischievous and capricious or who is trying to do his best to accommodate everyone but failing badly. We live our lives, we bump up against other people, all of us sin and make mistakes – and God watches it happen.

Now I know that as soon as I dare to say stuff like that I'm revealed as a closet deist. So let me say that of course God is interested in our lives: he does sustain them, he cares deeply about us and does from time to time 'intervene' to make things different for us. I don't buy the 'Divine Clockmaker', 'Great Architect of the Universe' belief that God created the world, set it running and then promptly forgot about it and left us all to get on with it. But neither am I finding it easy to join in with some of my friends who are desperately trying to ask, and seek some deep spiritual answer to, the question: 'Why did God allow your dream job to be snatched so cruelly from you?' The only answer I can come up with is that people have made mistakes in the past and I am paying for them, just as no doubt others pay for my mistakes.

I know this sounds a very negative and perhaps unsatisfying end to my odyssey, but I think it may be the case that my download from this experience is to realise afresh just how much I need God. If the world is, to a high degree, random, with little sense to be made of it, how much I need someone to turn to! If circumstances can kick me in the teeth, how good it is to have someone who will dry my tears, bind up my wounds and set me on my feet again to go back into the fray. This, I think, is the profound message of one of the Bible's greatest but most neglected books: the story of Job. The story begins with one blow after another to the poor chap: I know just a little of how that feels! What follows is chapter after chapter of philosophers trying to make sense of it. Finally God steps in again, firstly to remind the characters of just who he is, and then to show them the futility of their agonised questioning. Then Job gets it all back again, in spades, or at least the bits it is possible to get back. I believe that one day it will all come right as I meet my Lord face to face. I'd always thought that I would use that opportunity to sort out the stuff that I'd been confused about: why didn't I move to that place, why did I get ill, why did it all go so pear-shaped in Dorset, why *did* I get that job only to then not get it . . . But I'm wondering now whether those questions will be necessary, or whether they'll all get swept away for ever in that moment of supreme homecoming when I wake from the dreams and nightmares of this life and really begin to live. I'm still working out how that helps me to live now, but I think I'm appreciating more and more Paul's contention, 'that our present sufferings are not worth comparing with the glory that will be revealed in us' (Rom. 8:18). It has been said that Job didn't get any answers, but at the end he didn't have any questions either.

So here I am, recovering from serious illness, job-hunting but with no enthusiasm to put myself through parish ministry yet again, afraid of another spell of homelessness, but fortunately with a God who has never yet let me down and who will one day make sense of it all – not with answers but with himself. Let the last word come from a friend, a retired bishop who responded to the latest slap in the face with an e-mail that included these lines:

> Do I need to preach to you? You believe in Christ's victory, and have a strong leaning towards his guidance. So we look for the path to open.
>
> God's good hand be on you.

Amazingly, somehow I do still believe that it is.

Acknowledgements

It has been a while since I have published a book. I would like to thank Amy Boucher Pye, who had faith in me, who encouraged me, who nagged me (in a good way) and who has been so kind to me throughout the gestation and writing of this book. Sometimes you just need someone who can tell you that you can do it! Thanks too to Claire Musters and Becky Fawcett for their gentle but painstaking editing of the text: you will never know, dear reader, what atrocities their skills have saved you from. Thanks for medical advice from John Goepel, and for coffee and fry-ups to Dobbies Garden Centre, where much of this was written. And thanks to our many friends who have been such a support through the ups and downs of this journey.

Endnotes

1   The Dukan Diet, in case you're interested, and I haven't got a sponsorship deal, although I should have, being such a great evangelist for them.

2   C.S. Lewis, *The Problem of Pain* (London: Geoffrey Bles, 1940).

3   R. Rohr, *Falling Upward* (London: SPCK, 2012), p. 73.

4   You can buy the CD of the seminar here:
    https://www.essentialchristian.com/rt-rev-graham-cray/teaching/the-spiritual-gift-of-dissatisfaction-1-0

5   My favourite recording is the Deutsche Grammophon 1982 version with Claudio Abbado in St Albans Cathedral.

6   R. Rohr, *op. cit.* p. xvi.

7   R. Otto, *The Idea of the Holy* (London: Oxford University Press, 1923) You can now read this landmark book online at
    http://archive.org/stream/theideaoftheholy00ottouoft#page/n3/mode/2up

8   For a non-technical guide to the crazy world of therapy that is both amusing and profound I would recommend S. Sutherland, *Breakdown* (2nd edn, Oxford: Oxford University Press, 1998). You'll particularly enjoy the chapter on Orgone therapy. J. Kovel, *A Complete Guide to Therapy* (Harmondswoth: Penguin, 1979) is useful but less tongue-in-cheek.

9 My favourite Gestalt book is by Fritz Perls (its founder) *Gestalt Therapy Verbatim* (Boulder, Colorado: Real People, 1969) available as a download from http://www.2shared.com/document/BK_wvsiL/Gestalt_Therapy_Verbatim_PDF.html

10 For more details of their theories, see J. Westerhoff, *Will our Children Have Faith?* (New York: Seabury, 1976) and J. Fowler, *Weaving the New Creation* (New York: Harper Collins, 1991).

11 See C. and J. Leach, *And for your Children* (Crowborough: Monarch, 1994).

12 See R. Howard, *The Rise and Fall of the Nine O'Clock Service* (London: Mowbray, 1996) for a full and mostly accurate account of this tragic story.

13 To pursue this theme further, see C. Leach, *Keeping our Kids* (Cambridge: Grove, R30, 2007).

14 You can find the text here:
http://en.wikipedia.org/wiki/Te_Deum

15 You can find the full text here:
http://www.methodist.org.uk/who-we-are/what-is-distinctive-about-methodism/a-covenant-with-god

16 J. Leach, *Ending Well: How to Close Things Down* (Cambridge: Grove R39, 2010).

17 J. Witcombe and J. Leach, *Hanging on to God* (Cambridge: Grove R33, 2008).

18 The 'Mortymer Trilogy' by Alexander Cordell, three novels set within what is now Monmouth Diocese, give a sometimes harrowing account of life in nineteenth-century Welsh mining communities. The novels are *Rape of the Fair Country* (1959), *The Hosts of Rebecca* (1960) and *Song of the Earth* (1969). All books published in Llanfoist by Blorenge Books.

[19] There is a really helpful chapter on adult bullying, with a useful bibliography, in B. Geary, and J. Bryan, *Christian Handbook of Abuse, Addiction and Difficult Behaviour* (Stowmarket: Kevin Mayhew, 2008).

[20] S. Tracy. 'Sexual Abuse and Forgiveness' *Journal of Psychology and Theology* Vol. 27, No. 3 (1999): p. 291ff.

[21] See for example http://www.thelancet.com/journals/lanonc/article/PIIS1470-2045%2804%2901597-9/fulltext for an exploration of the roles of stress and depression in cancer.

[22] Excerpted from *The Power to Heal* by Francis MacNutt, Copyright 1977 by Ave Maria Press, P.O. Box 428, Notre Dame, IN 46556. Used with permission of the publisher.

[23] By an amazing coincidence Chris and I do not just share the same birthday: our wedding anniversary is the same too!

[24] I'd need to check this out, but I'm not sure there is a great deal of medical evidence to suggest that silly socks do actually prevent chest infections.

[25] In case you can't make it that day it's the Ferry Corsten Remix of William Orbit's version of Barber's *Adagio for Strings*.

[26] W.H. Vanstone, *The Stature of Waiting* (London: DLT, 1982).

Exposing the Psalms

Unmasking their beauty, art, and power for a new generation

Peter Nevland

Exposing the Psalms unlocks the symbolism and artistry of the ancient Psalms. The first in his Tree of Psalms series, Peter Nevland's stories plunge you into their ancient beauty and expose their relevance to twenty-first-century life. This is an unusual and entertaining commentary on thirty psalms, written with a fresh, colloquial and post-modern voice. Each chapter ends with follow-up questions and a poem written by the author – a lyrical exploration of some of the ideas of the psalm, which is, of course, itself a lyrical medium.

His follow-up questions get youth, college, and adult church groups talking. His palm-inspired poetry will unhinge your heart. Feel the Psalms like you've never felt them before. Gaze in awe at the God they reveal. You just might create your own psalm-inspired art.

978-1-86024-903-7

Authentic

We trust you enjoyed reading this book
from Authentic Media. If you want to be
informed of any new titles from this author
and other exciting releases you can sign up
to the Authentic newsletter online:

authenticmedia.co.uk

Contact us:

By post:
Authentic Media
52 Presley Way
Crownhill
Milton Keynes
MK8 0ES

E-mail:
info@authenticmedia.co.uk

Follow us: